AUTHENTIC TRANSCRIPTIONS
WITH NOTES AND TABLATURE

DAVID LEE ROTH
AND THE SONGS OF
VAN HALEN

ISBN 978-1-4234-3618-8

In Australia Contact:
Hal Leonard Australia Pty. Ltd.
4 Lentara Court
Cheltenham, Victoria, 3192 Australia
Email: ausadmin@halleonard.com.au

HAL•LEONARD®
CORPORATION

7777 W. BLUEMOUND RD. P.O. BOX 13819 MILWAUKEE, WI 53213

Visit Hal Leonard Online at
www.halleonard.com

from *Van Halen*

Ain't Talkin' 'Bout Love

Words and Music by David Lee Roth, Edward Van Halen, Alex Van Halen and Michael Anthony

*Tune down 1/2 step:
(low to high) E♭-A♭-D♭-G♭-B♭-E♭

Intro
Moderate Rock ♩ = 138

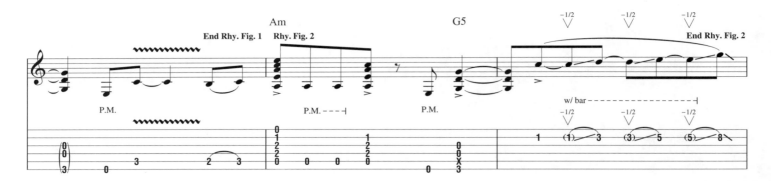

*Recording sounds 1/4 step sharp.
**Chord symbols reflect basic harmony.
†Set echo at approx. 100ms delay.
Set flanger for slow speed w/ regeneration
sweep and moderate depth.

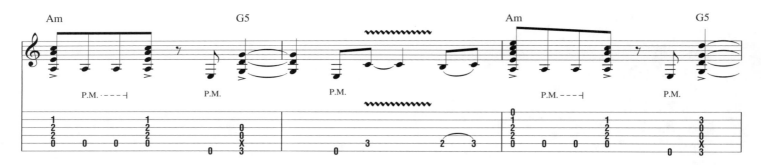

1. I heard the news, ba - by, all a - bout your dis - ease.
look - in', and on the streets a - gain.

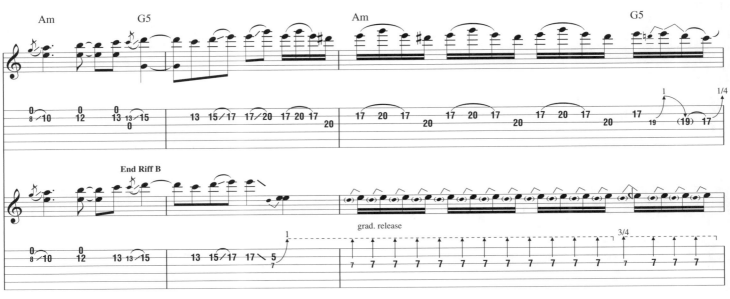

Chorus
Gtr. 1: w/ Rhy. Fig. 1 (3 times)
Gtr. 2 tacet

Ain't talk-in' 'bout love.   Babe, it's a rot-ten to the core. ___

Ain't talk - in' 'bout love.   Just like I told you be - fore, ___

Interlude

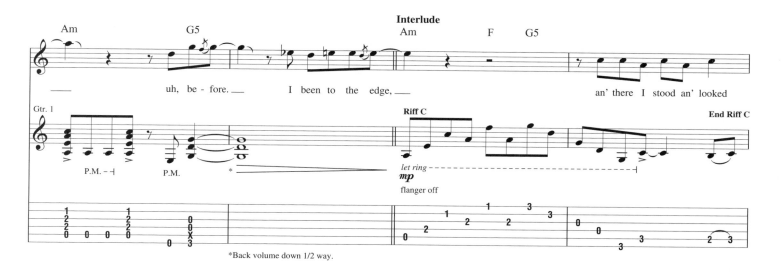

___   uh, be - fore. ___   I been to the edge, ___   an' there I stood an' looked

*Back volume down 1/2 way.

Gtr. 1: w/ Riff C (2 times)

down. ___   You know I lost a lot of friends _ there, ___ ba - by,   I got no time to mess a -

round.   Mmm, _ so if you want it, got to bleed for it, ba - by.   Yeah,   got to, got to

bleed,   ba - by.   Mmm, _ you got to, got to bleed,   ba - by.   Hey,   got to, got to

Pitches: D G B

Chorus

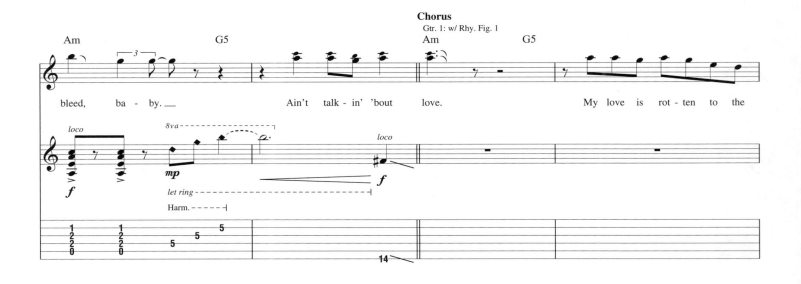

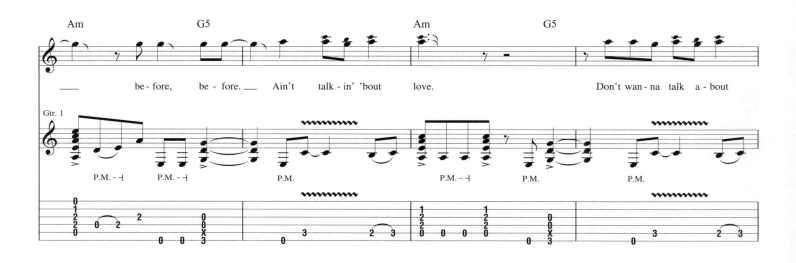

from *Women and Children First*

And the Cradle Will Rock

Words and Music by David Lee Roth, Edward Van Halen, Alex Van Halen and Michael Anthony

Intro
Moderately ♩ = 107

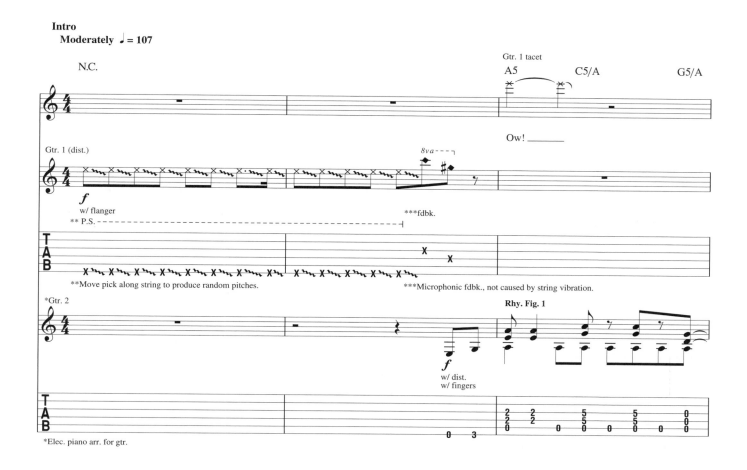

*Elec. piano arr. for gtr.

**Move pick along string to produce random pitches.

***Microphonic fdbk., not caused by string vibration.

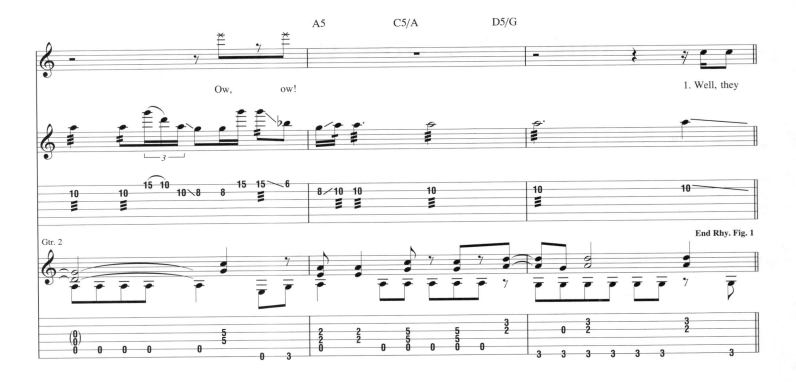

Verse

say it's kind __ a fright - 'nin' how __ this young - er gen - er - a - tion swings. You know, it's

more than just some new sen - sa - tion. Well, the kid is in - to los - in' sleep, __ and he

*Vol. swell
**Microphonic fdbk., not caused by string vibration.

Chorus
Gtr. 1 tacet
Gtr. 2: w/ Rhy. Fig. 1
Gtr. 3: w/ Riff A

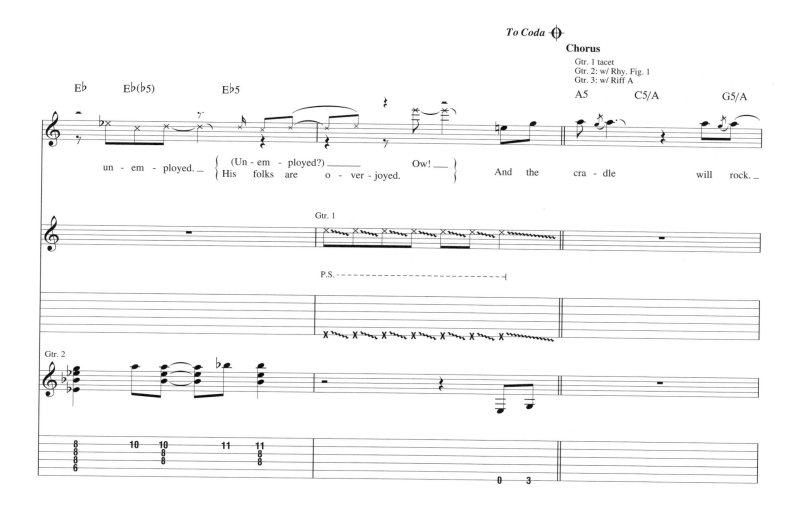

Eb   Eb(b5)   Eb5   A5   C5/A   G5/A

un - em - ployed. _ { (Un - em - ployed?) ____ Ow! _ } And the cra - dle will rock. _
His folks are o - ver - joyed.

Gtr. 1

P.S. - - - - - - - - - - - - - - - - - -

Gtr. 2

A5   C5/A   D5/G

_ Ow! _ And the cra - dle, the cra - dle will rock. ___ And I ___ say

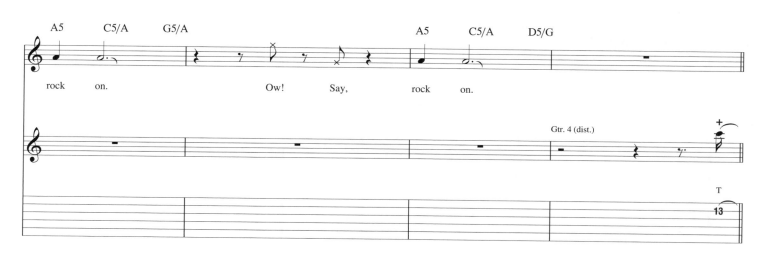

A5   C5/A   G5/A   A5   C5/A   D5/G

rock   on.   Ow!   Say,   rock   on.

Gtr. 4 (dist.)

Guitar Solo

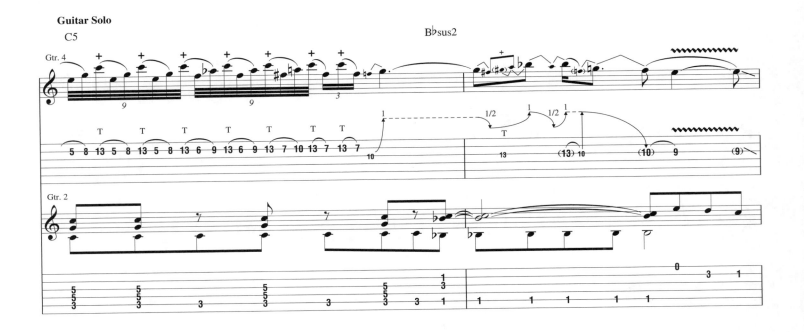

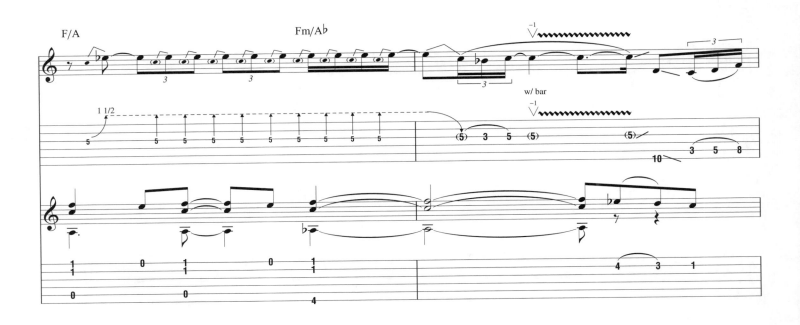

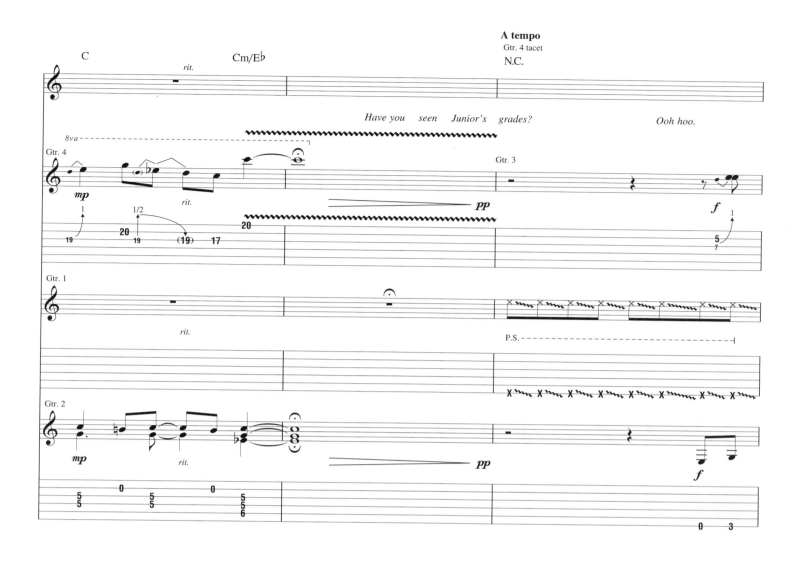

Have you seen Junior's grades?

Ooh hoo.

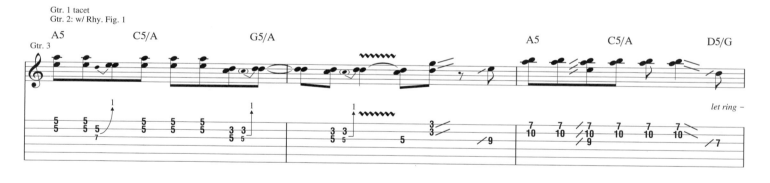

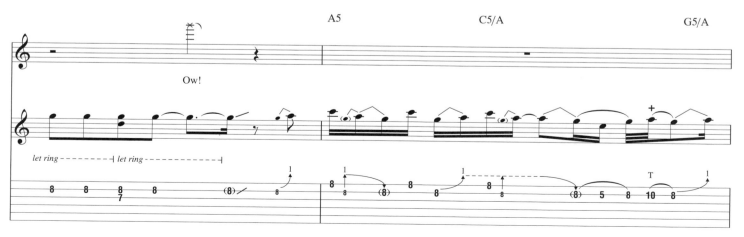

Ow!

15

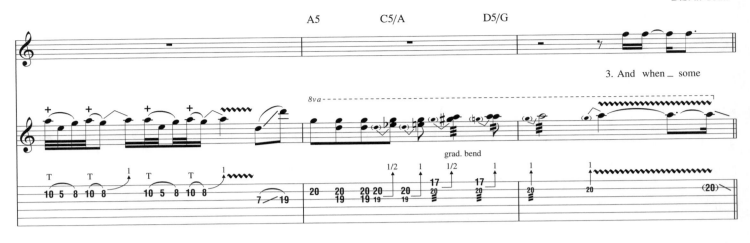

3. And when __ some

⊕ Coda
Chorus

Gtr. 1 tacet
Gtr. 2: w/ Rhy. Fig. 1
Gtr. 3: w/ Riff A (1st 4 meas.)

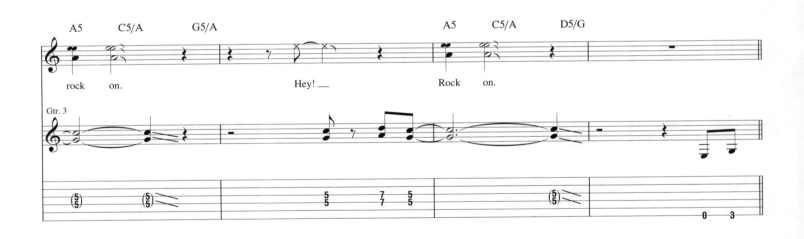

cra - dle   will rock. ___   Yes, the cra - dle,   cra - dle will rock. _____   I say

rock   on.   Hey! ___   Rock   on.

Outro
Gtr. 1: w/ Rhy. Fig. 1 (till fade)   w/ Lead Voc. ad lib. (till fade)

Rock   on.   Rock   on. ___   (Rock   on!

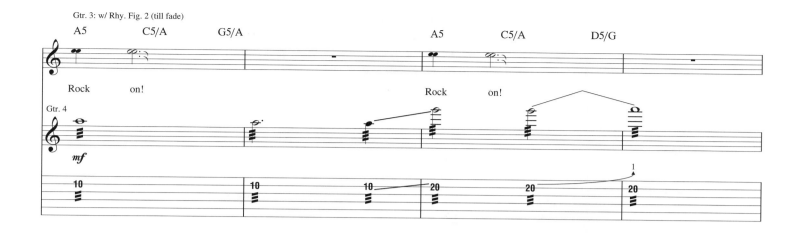

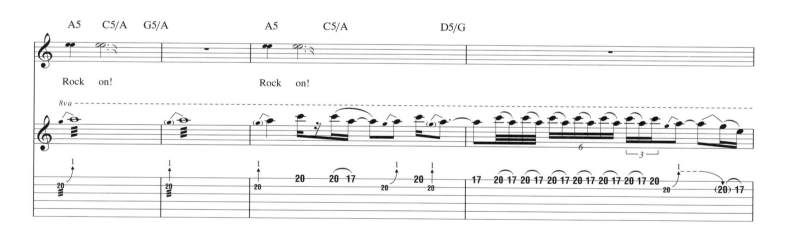

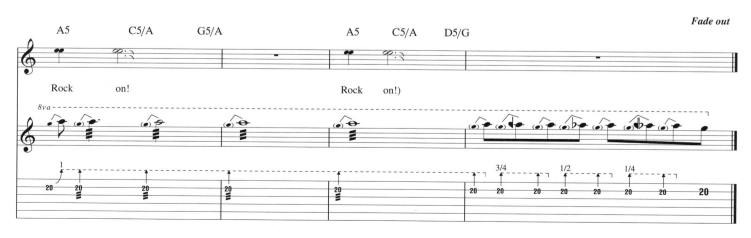

from *Van Halen*

Beautiful Girls

Words and Music by David Lee Roth, Edward Van Halen, Alex Van Halen and Michael Anthony

Tune down 1/2 step:
(low to high) Eb-Ab-Db-Gb-Bb-Eb

Intro
Moderately ♩ = 104

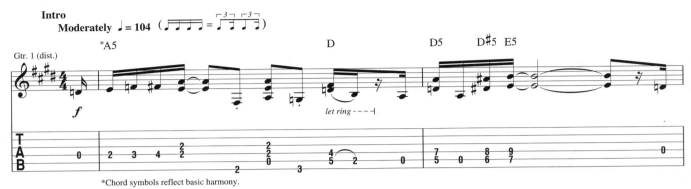

*Chord symbols reflect basic harmony.

1. She was a

Copyright © 1979 Diamond Dave Music, WB Music Corp. and Van Halen Music
All Rights for Diamond Dave Music Administered by Red Stripe Plane Music, LLC
All Rights for Van Halen Music Administered by WB Music Corp.
All Rights Reserved   Used by Permission

sweet talk-in' hon-ey with a lit-tle bit o' mon-ey, she turn ___ your head a-round.) ___

Crea-ture

from the sea ___ with the looks to me ___ like she'd like to fool a-round. ___ What a

snap-py lit-tle mam-my, gon-na keep her pap-py hap-py and ac-com-pa-ny me, ___ to the ends of the ___

___ Earth, ___ ah, ___ yeah. ___ A, that's what I said.

*Played as even sixteenth-notes.

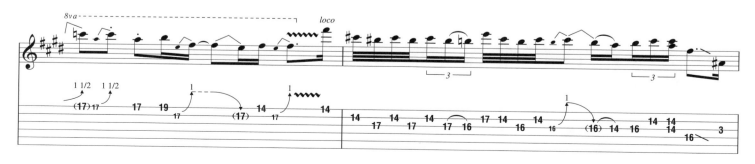

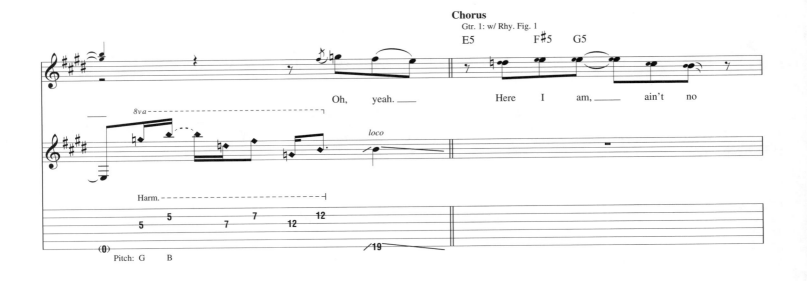

Chorus
Gtr. 1: w/ Rhy. Fig. 1

Oh, yeah. ___ Here I am, ___ ain't no

man of the world, ___ no. ___ All I need ___ is a beau-ti-ful girl. ___

Ah ___ yeah. Whoa, I ain't ___ ly - in' to ___
(Ah yeah, beau-ti-ful girls.

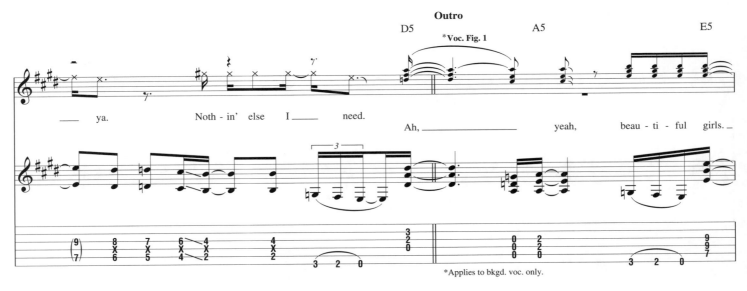

Outro

___ ya. Noth - in' else I ___ need. Ah, ___ yeah, beau-ti-ful girls. ___

*Applies to bkgd. voc. only.

*Kissing sound

from *1984*

Hot for Teacher

Words and Music by David Lee Roth, Edward Van Halen, Alex Van Halen and Michael Anthony

*Pickup selector set to bridge pickup, w/ vol. control set to full vol.

**Chord symbols reflect implied harmony.

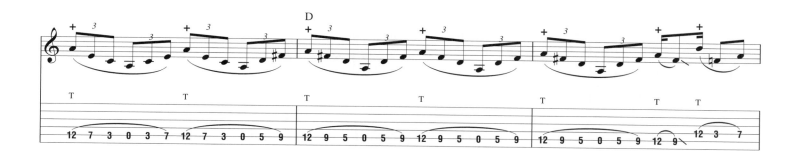

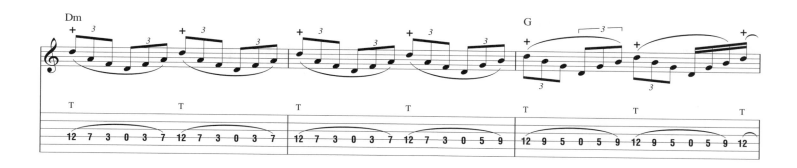

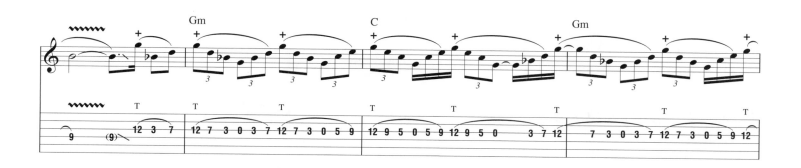

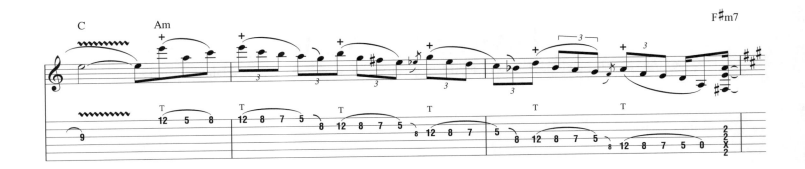

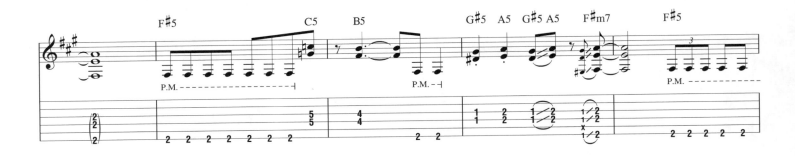

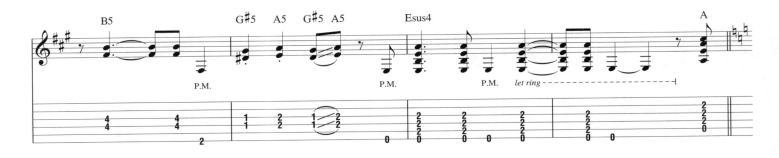

𝄋 Interlude
w/ classroom noise

Spoken: Hey, I heard you missed us, we're back!
Spoken: Ah, man, I think the clock is

*Switch to neck pickup, w/ vol. control set to 1/2 vol.

wow, ___ man, ___ I said...
Hey!
slow.

Wait a ___
I brought my

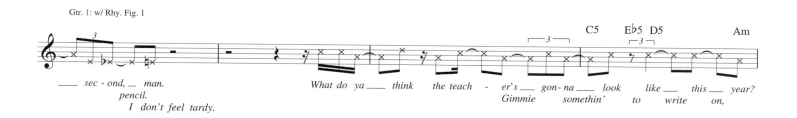

___ sec - ond, ___ man.
pencil.
I don't feel tardy.

What do ya ___ think the teach - er's gon-na ___ look like ___ this ___ year?
Gimmie somethin' to write on,

man!

Oh! ___
Oh!
Class

(Uh!)
Uh!
dismissed!

*Switch to bridge pickup.

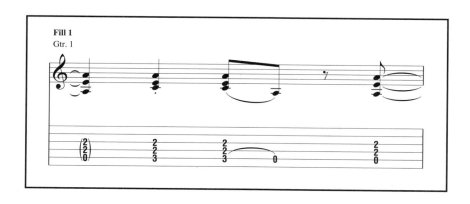

Fill 1

31

Chorus
Gtr. 1: w/ Rhy. Fig. 2 (3 times)

got it bad, ___ got it bad. ___ I'm hot for teach - er. ___

C5 Eb5 D5   Am

C5 Eb5 D5   Am

I've got it bad, ___ so ___ bad. ___ I'm hot for teach -

C5 Eb5 D5   Am

D.S. al Coda 1

E   Esus4   A5

- er. ___

Gtr. 1

P.M. - - - -

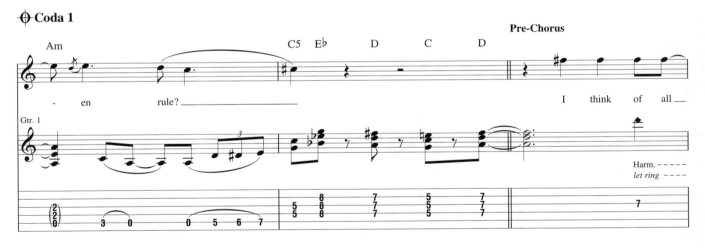

⊕ Coda 1

Pre-Chorus

Am   C5 Eb   D   C   D

- en   rule? _____   I think of all ___

Gtr. 1

Harm. - - - - -
let ring - - - -

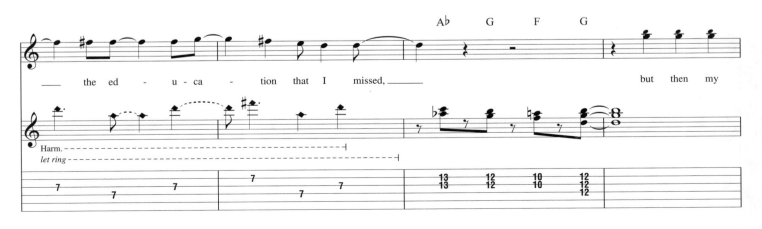

___ the ed - u - ca - tion that I missed, _____   but then my

Ab   G   F   G

Harm. -
let ring - - -

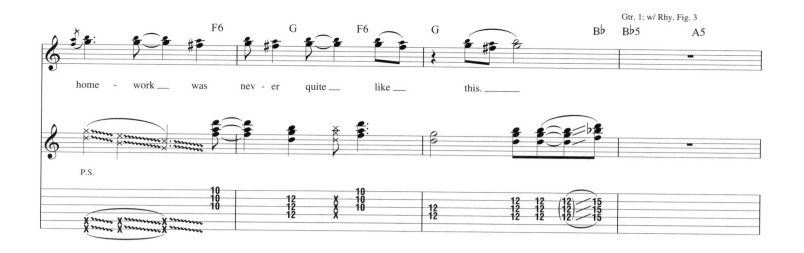

home - work ___ was nev - er quite ___ like ___ this. ___

Chorus

Gtr. 1: w/ Rhy. Fig. 2 (3 times)

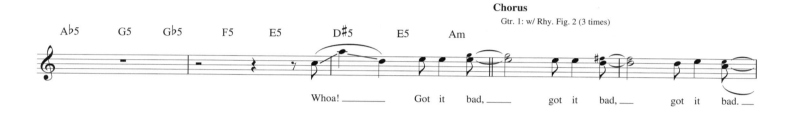

Whoa! ___ Got it bad, ___ got it bad, ___ got it bad. ___

I'm hot for teach - er. ___

I've got it bad, ___ so bad. ___ I'm hot for teach -

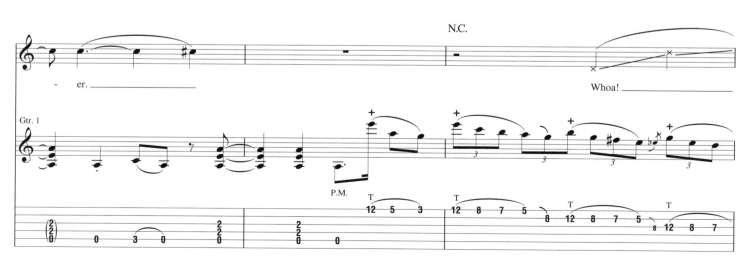

- er. ___ Whoa! ___

Guitar Solo

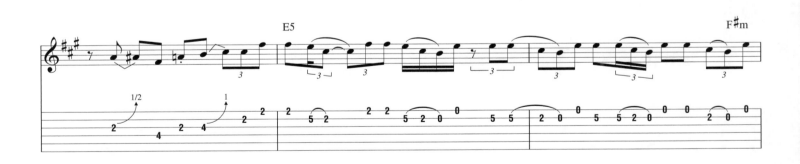

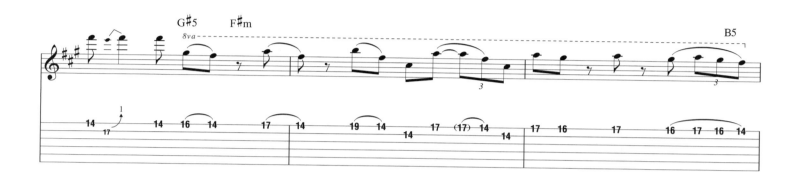

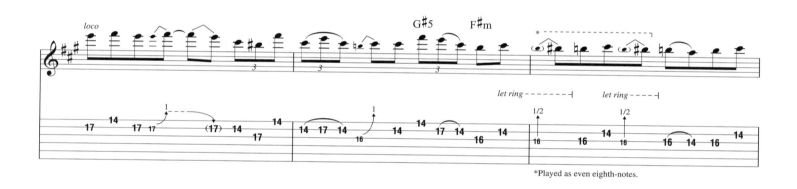

*Played as even eighth-notes.

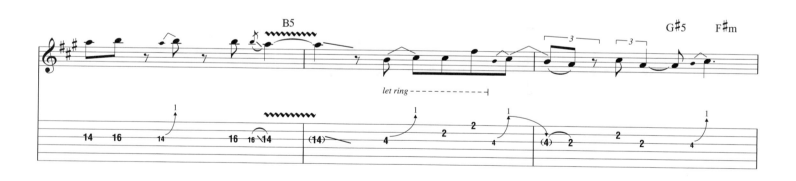

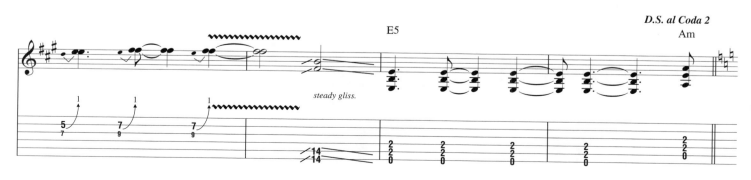

37

Chorus

I've got it bad, _____ got it bad, got it bad. _____

I'm hot for teach - er. _____ Oh!

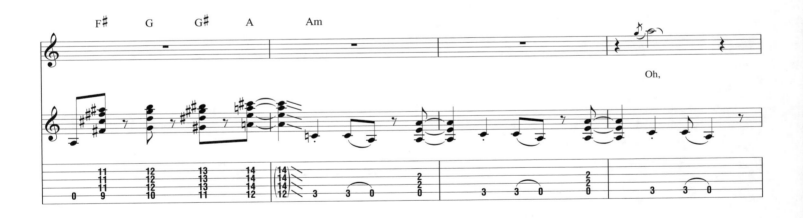

Oh,

yes ___ I'm hot! ___ Wow! _____

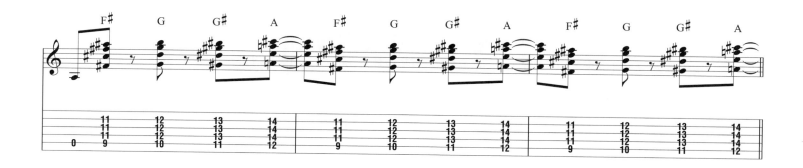

Outro
Free time

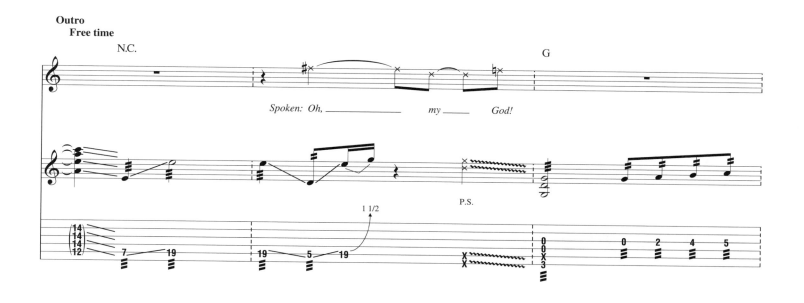

Spoken: Oh, _____ my ___ God!

Whoo!

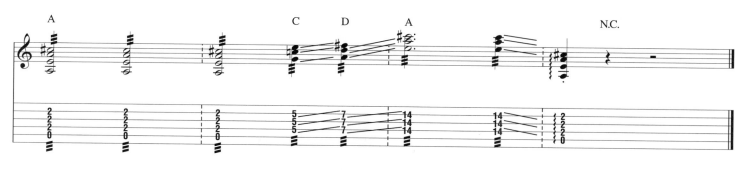

from *Diver Down*

Cathedral

Words and Music by David Lee Roth, Edward Van Halen, Alex Van Halen and Michael Anthony

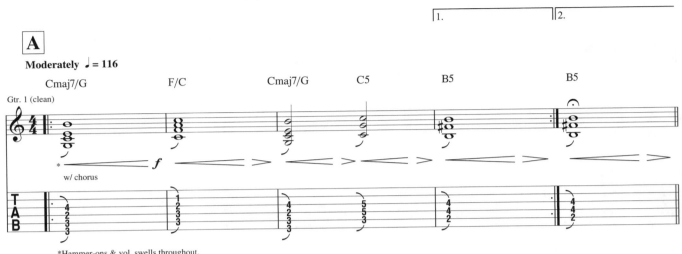

*Hammer-ons & vol. swells throughout.

**Chord symbols reflect implied harmony.

***Set for dotted-eighth note regeneration w/ 1 repeat.

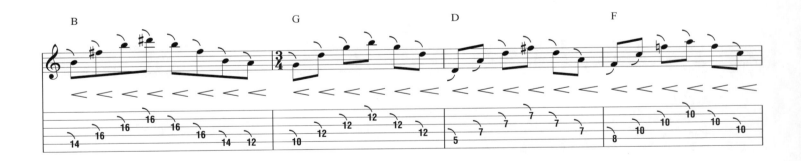

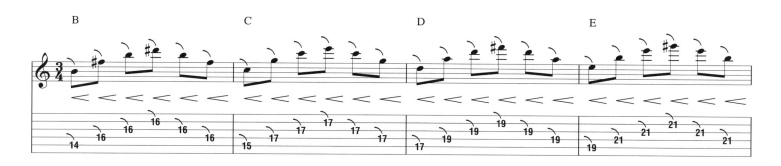

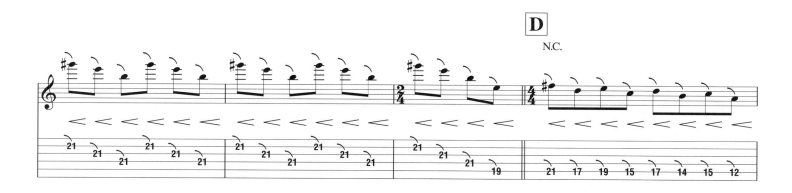

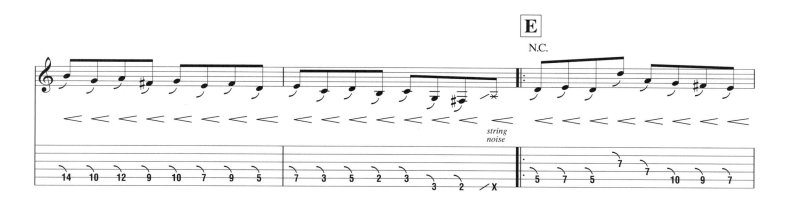

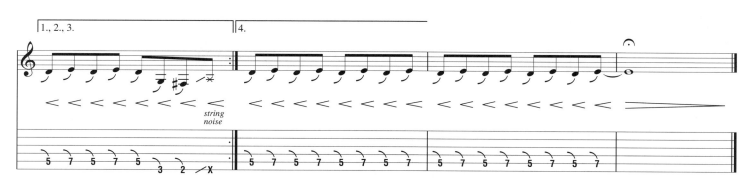

Dance the Night Away

Words and Music by David Lee Roth, Edward Van Halen, Alex Van Halen and Michael Anthony

Tune down 1/2 step:
(low to high) Eb-Ab-Db-Gb-Bb-Eb

Intro
Moderately ♩ = 129

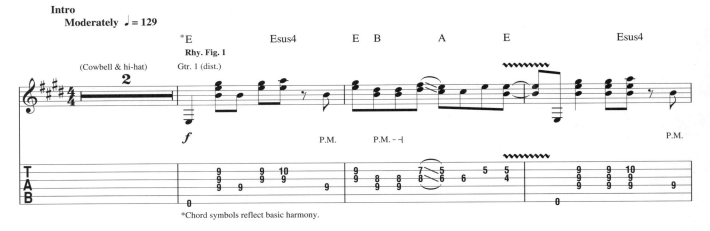

*Chord symbols reflect basic harmony.

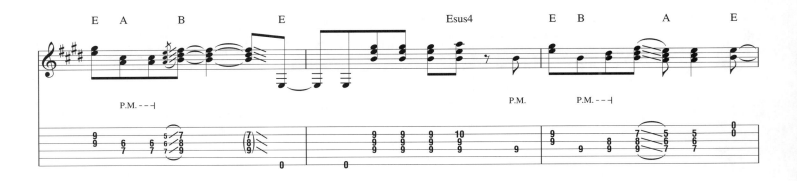

Verse

1. Have you   seen _____ her? _____   So _____

Chorus

Gtr. 1: w/ Rhy. Fig. 1

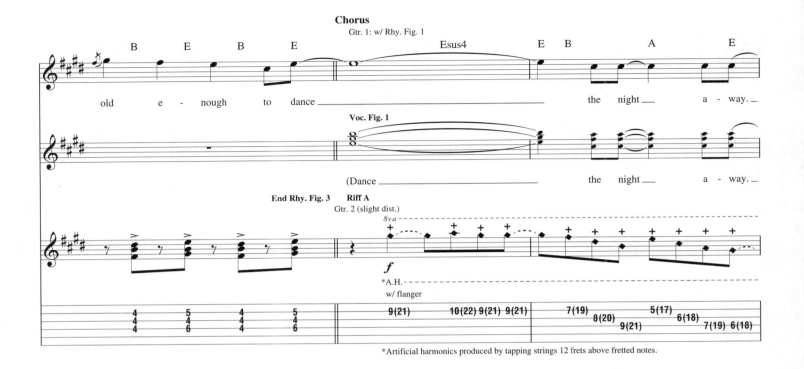

old e - nough to dance _____ the night _____ a - way. _____

Voc. Fig. 1

(Dance _____ the night _____ a - way.

End Rhy. Fig. 3   Riff A
Gtr. 2 (slight dist.)

*A.H.
w/ flanger

*Artificial harmonics produced by tapping strings 12 frets above fretted notes.

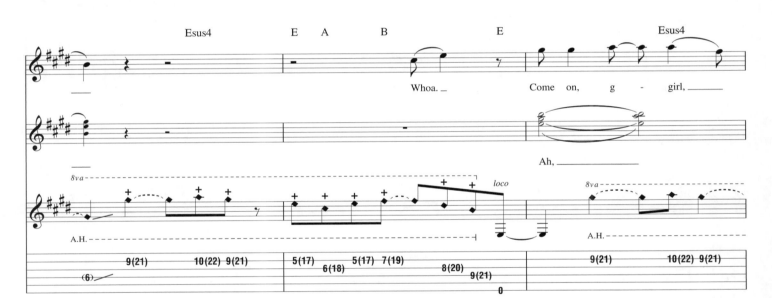

Whoa. _____   Come on, g - girl, _____

Ah,

2. A live

End Voc. Fig. 1

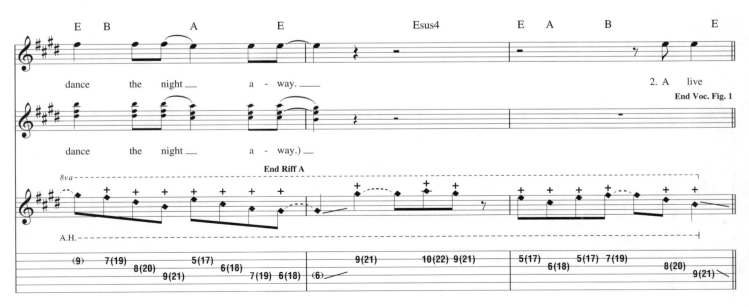

dance the night _____ a - way. _____

dance the night _____ a - way.) _____

End Riff A

Verse

wire, ___ bare - ly a be - gin - ner, but just watch that la - dy go. ___ She's on

fire ___ 'cause danc - in' gets her high - er than, uh, an - y - thing else she ___ knows. ___

Pre-Chorus

Oo, ___ won't ya turn your head my ___ way? ___
(Oo, ba - by, ba - by.

Gtr. 1: w/ Rhy. Fig. 3

Oo, ___ Well, don't skip ro - mance ___ 'cause you're old e - nough to dance ___
Oo, ba - by, ba - by.)

Chorus
Bkgd. Voc: w/ Voc. Fig. 1
Gtr. 1: w/ Rhy. Fig. 1 (1st 6 meas.)
Gtr. 2: w/ Riff A

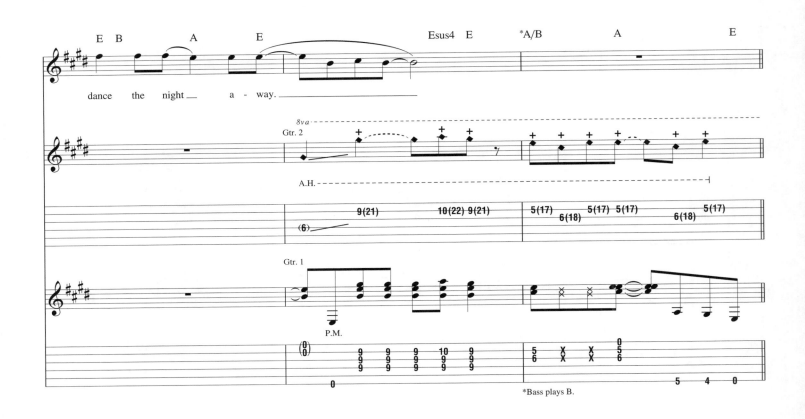

*Bass plays B.

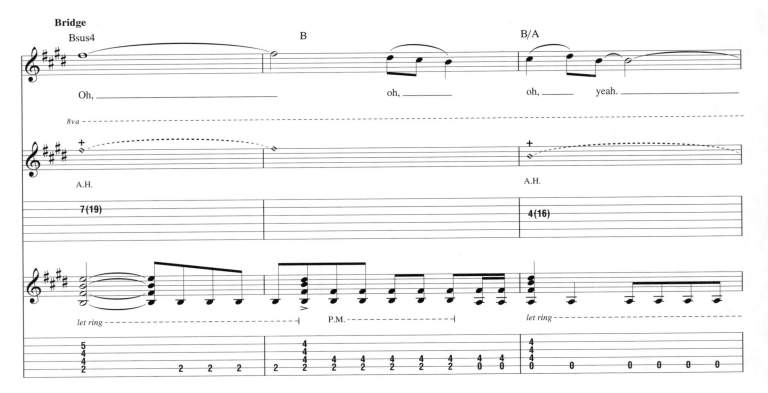

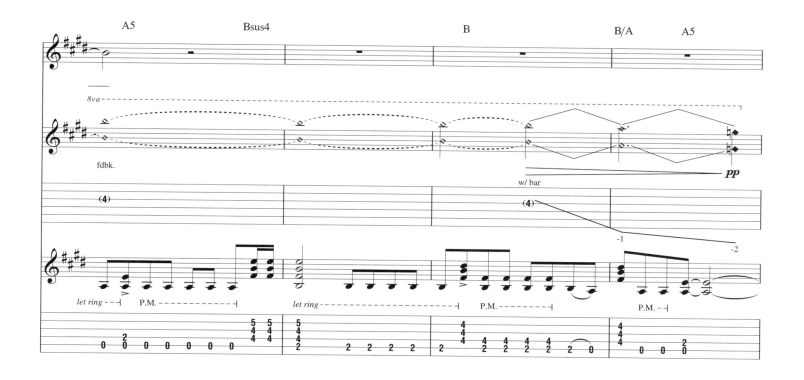

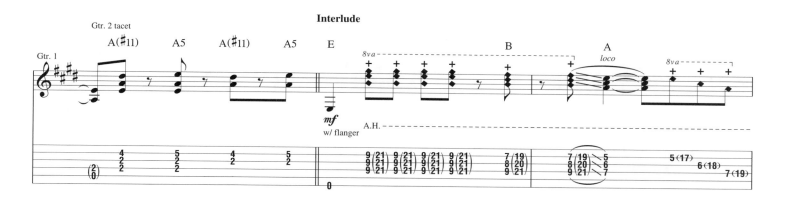

Interlude

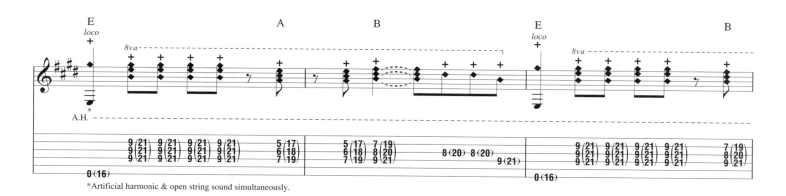

*Artificial harmonic & open string sound simultaneously.

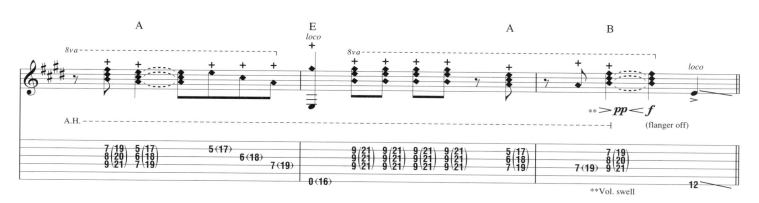

**Vol. swell

Outro-Chorus

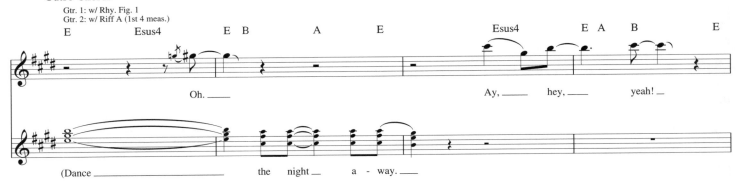

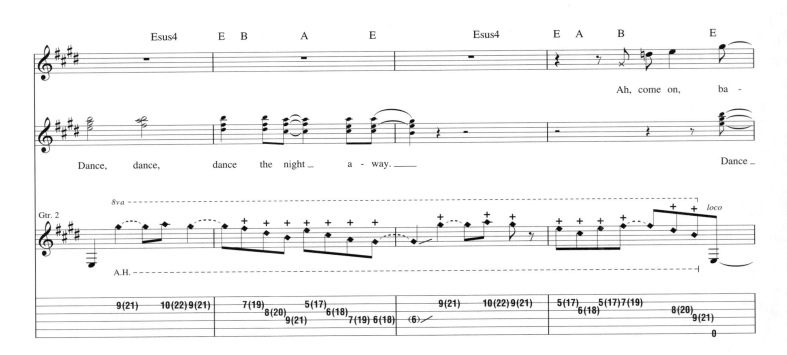

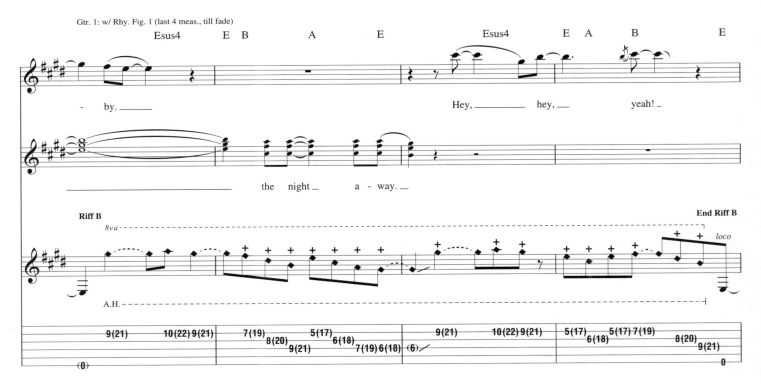

Gtr. 2: w/ Riff B (till fade)

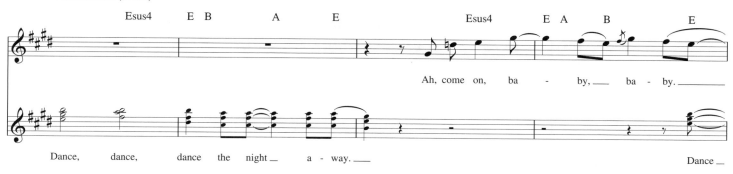

Ah, come on, ba - by, ___ ba - by. ___

Dance, dance, dance the night ___ a - way. ___ Dance ___

Begin fade

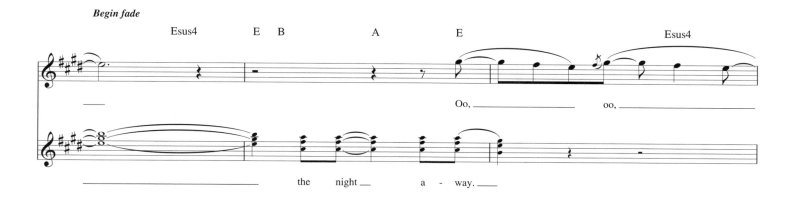

Oo, ___ oo, ___

___ the night ___ a - way. ___

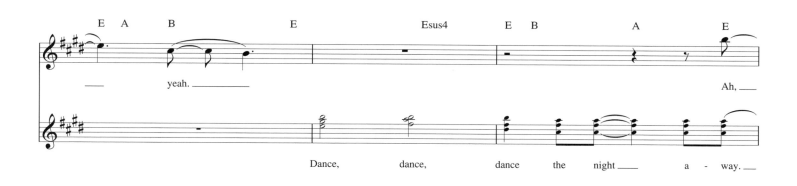

___ yeah. ___ Ah, ___

Dance, dance, dance the night ___ a - way. ___

Fade out

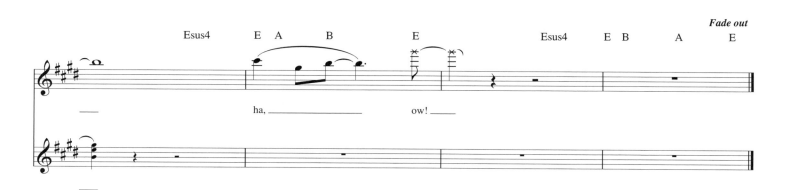

ha, ___ ow! ___

from *Van Halen II*

D.O.A.

Words and Music by David Lee Roth, Edward Van Halen, Alex Van Halen and Michael Anthony

Tune down 1/2 step:
(low to high) E♭-A♭-D♭-G♭-B♭-E♭

Intro
Moderately ♩ = 137
Free time

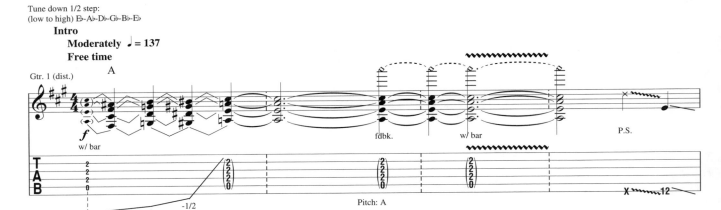

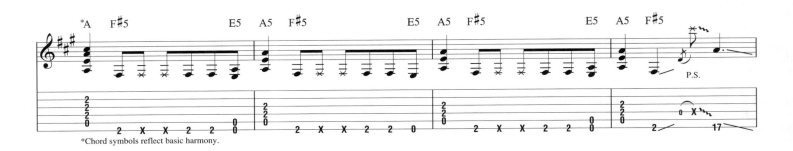

*Chord symbols reflect basic harmony.

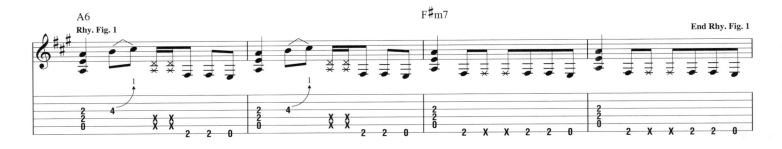

1. We was

Verse

broke and hun-gry on a sum-mer day. ___ They sent the

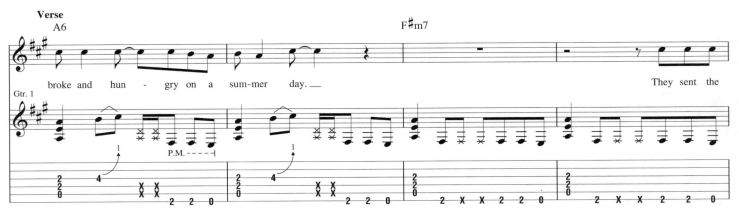

Gtr. 1: w/ Rhy. Fig. 1

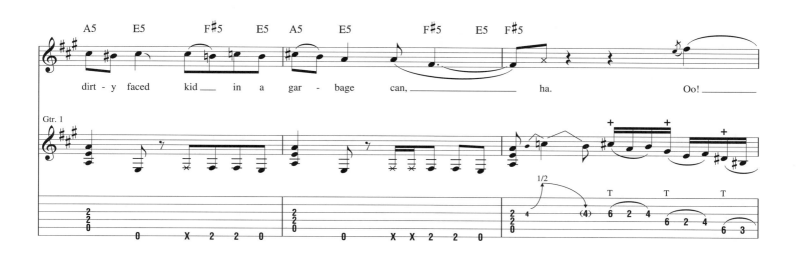

Pre-Chorus

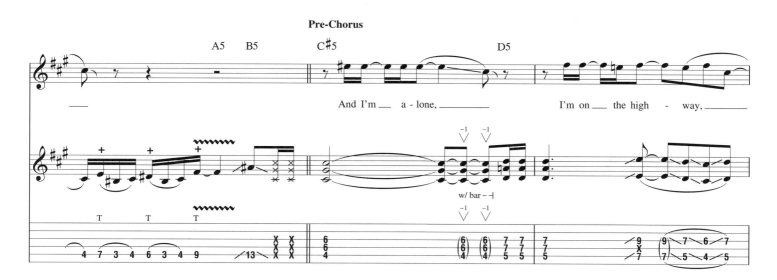

*Bends, releases & vibrato executed w/ left hand ring finger at 4th fret.

52

may - or down ____ in his pick - up truck.   The ju - ry

look at me, ____ say, ____ "Out - ta luck."   Oo, _____

Pre-Chorus

____ yeah!   And I'm a - lone, _____   I'm on the high - way, ____

Chorus

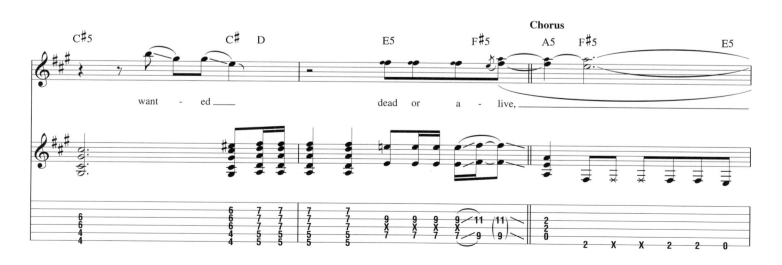

want - ed ____   dead or a - live, _____

dead or a - live. _____ Uh, ah! _____

w/ bar

Guitar Solo

Gtr. 1

slight P.H.------

w/ bar

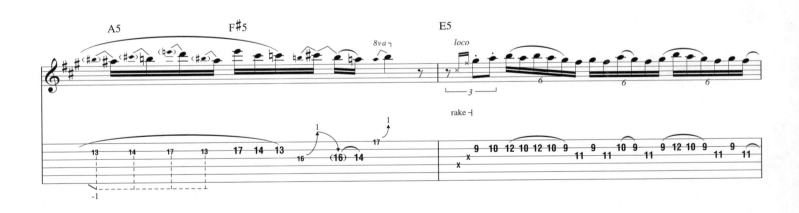

loco

rake

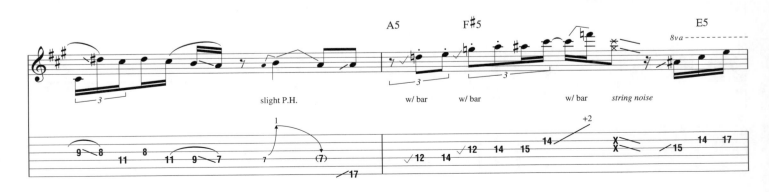

slight P.H.

w/ bar   w/ bar   w/ bar   string noise

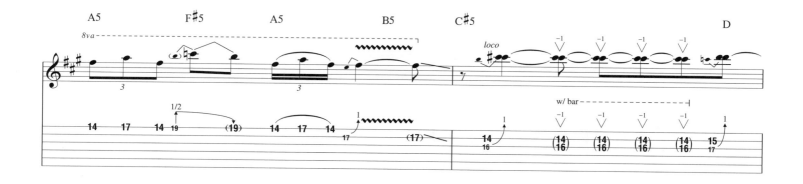

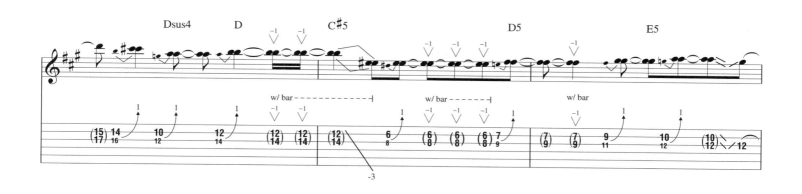

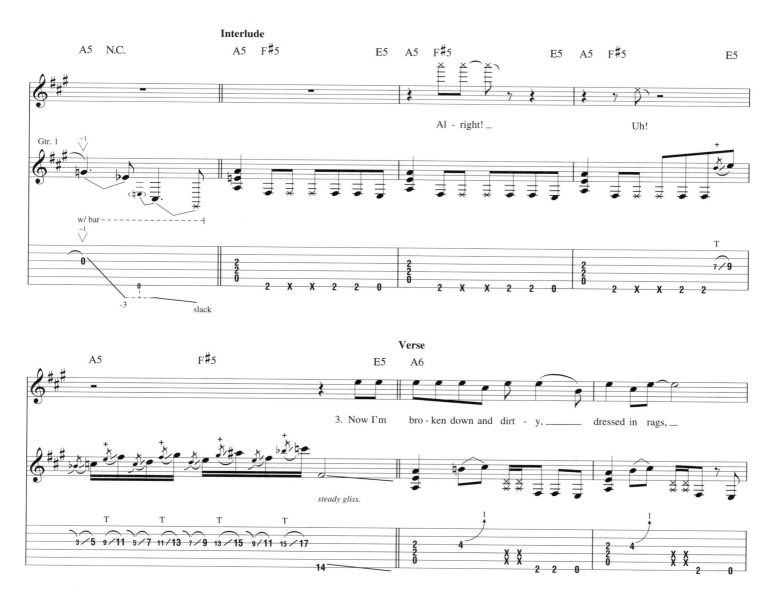

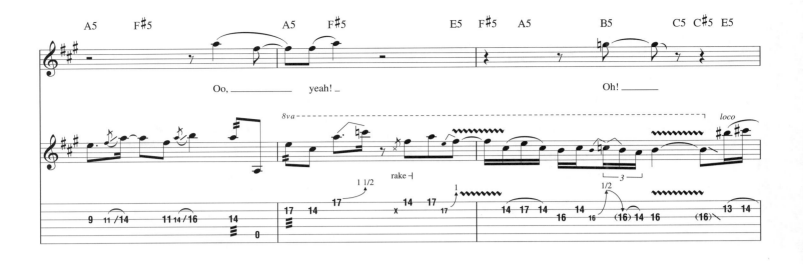

Oo, _____ yeah! _

Oh! _____

*Played ahead of the beat.

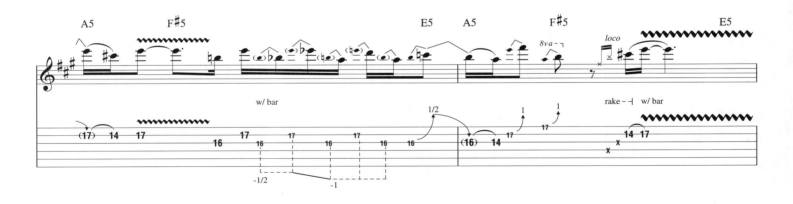

Outro

Gtr. 1: w/ Rhy. Fig. 1 (2 1/2 times)

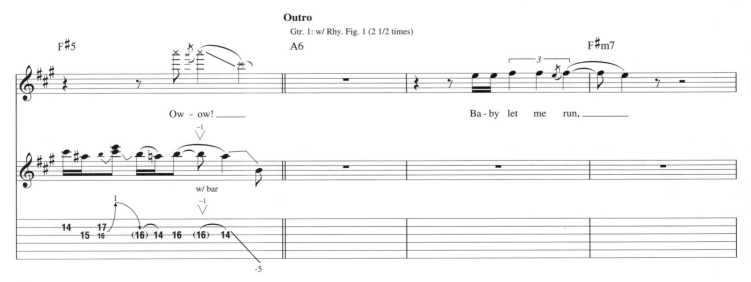

Ow - ow! _____

Ba - by let me run, _____

yeah, ___ yeah! ___

I'm a spark on the ho-ri-zon. ___

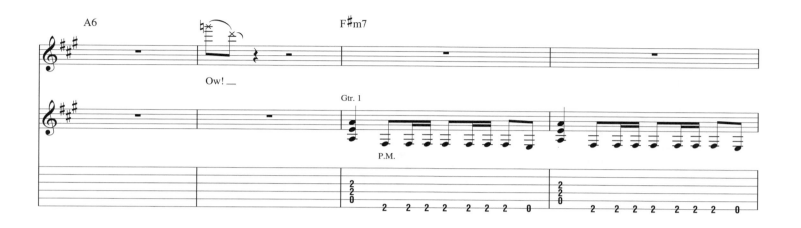

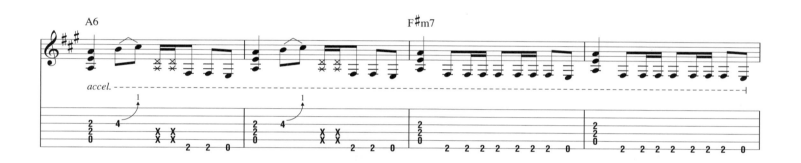

Faster ♩ = 167

Gtr. 1: w/ Rhy. Fig. 2

Da, da, da, da, da, da, dow!

Da, da, da, da, dow!

Repeat and fade

from *1984*

Drop Dead Legs

Words and Music by David Lee Roth, Edward Van Halen, Alex Van Halen and Michael Anthony

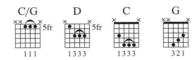

Drop D tuning:
(low to high) D-A-D-G-B-E

Intro
Moderately ♩ = 90

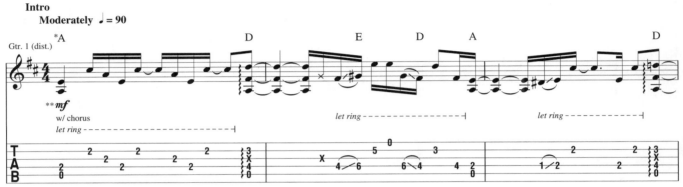

*Chord symbols reflect implied harmony.

**Volume knob at 1/2.

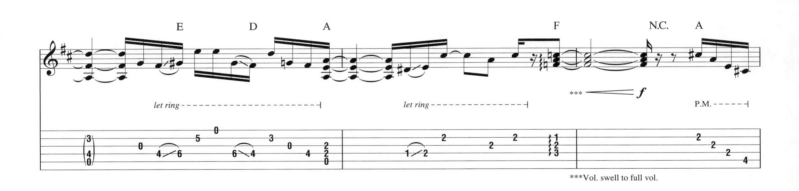

***Vol. swell to full vol.

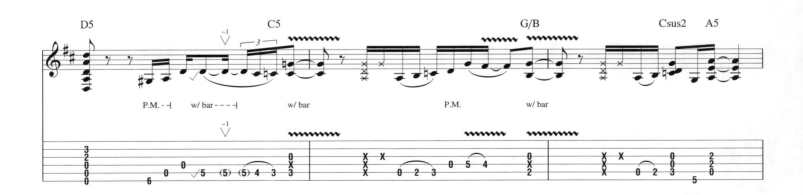

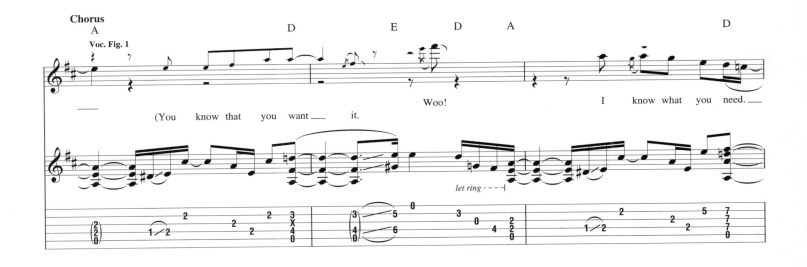

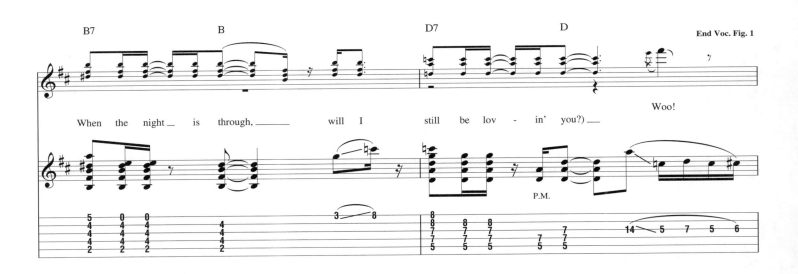

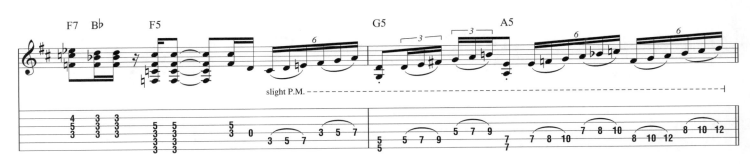

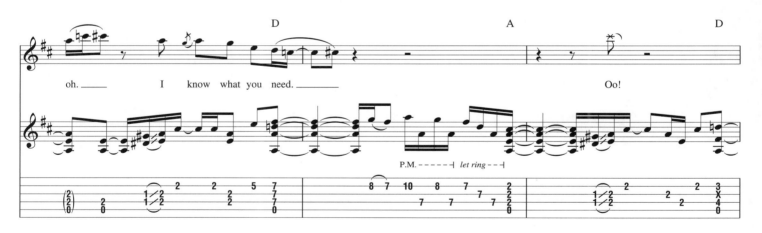

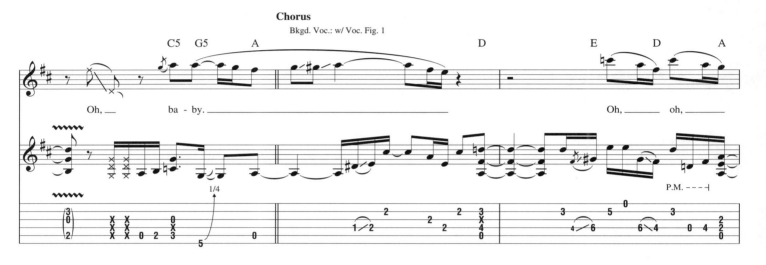

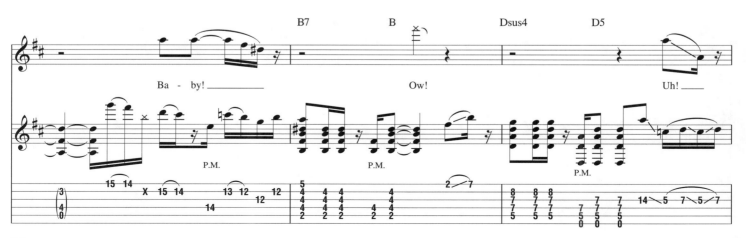

Interlude

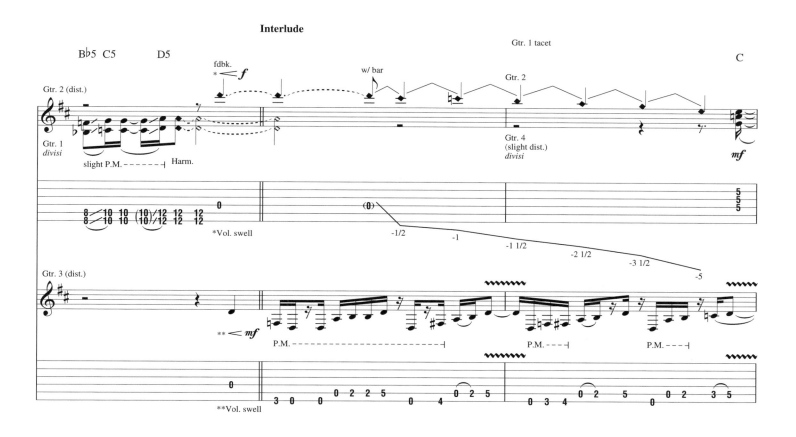

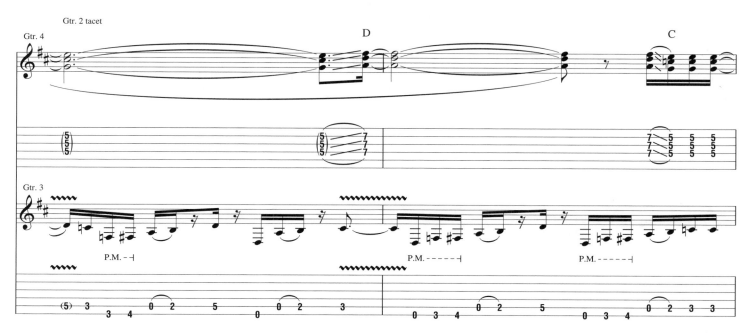

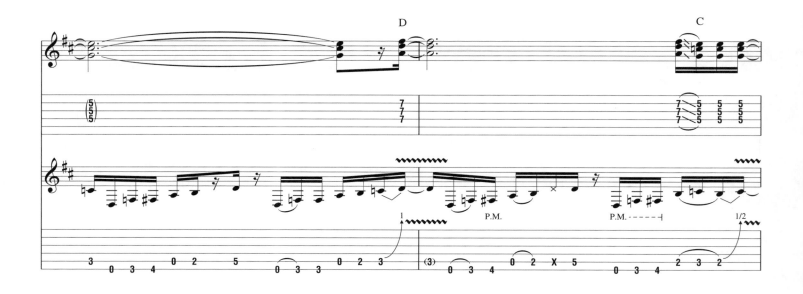

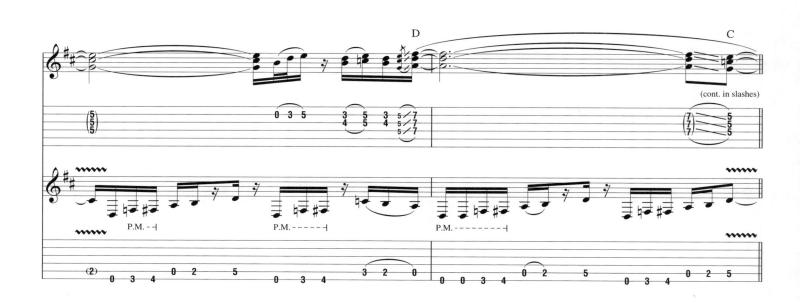

Outro-Guitar Solo

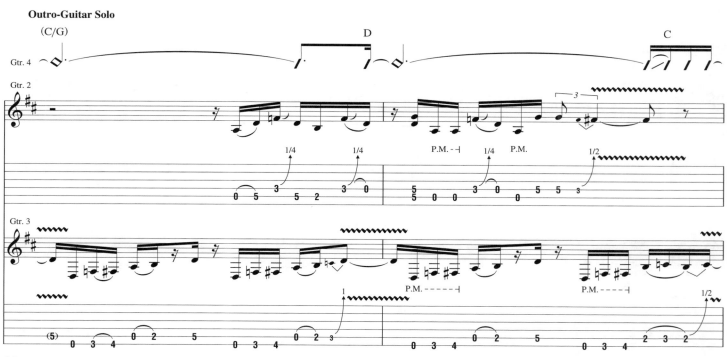

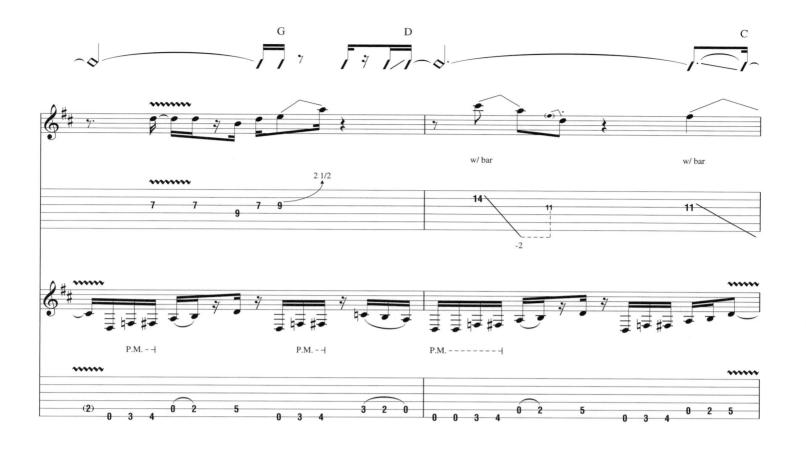

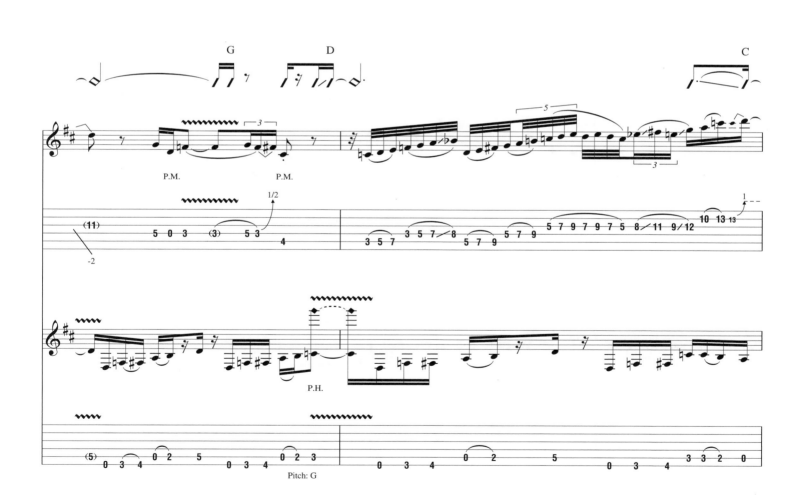

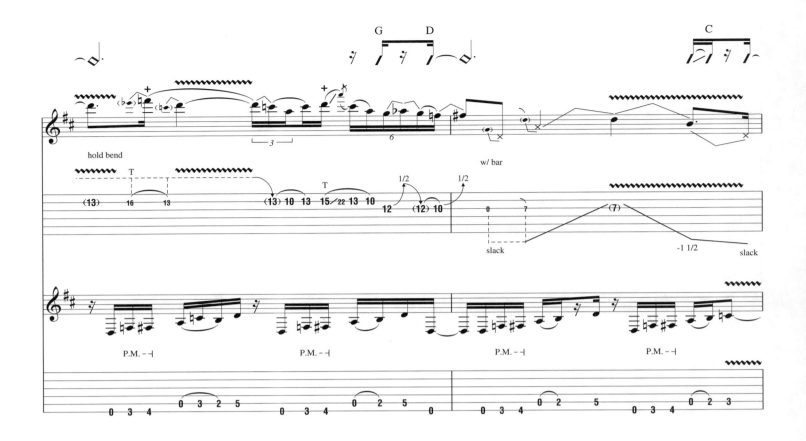

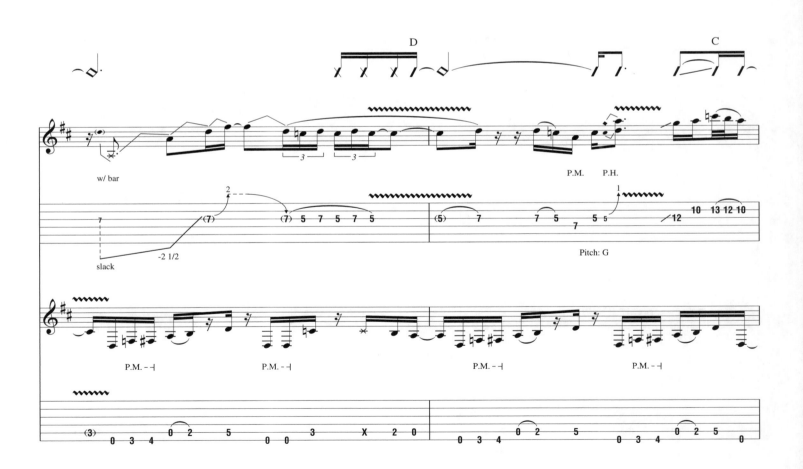

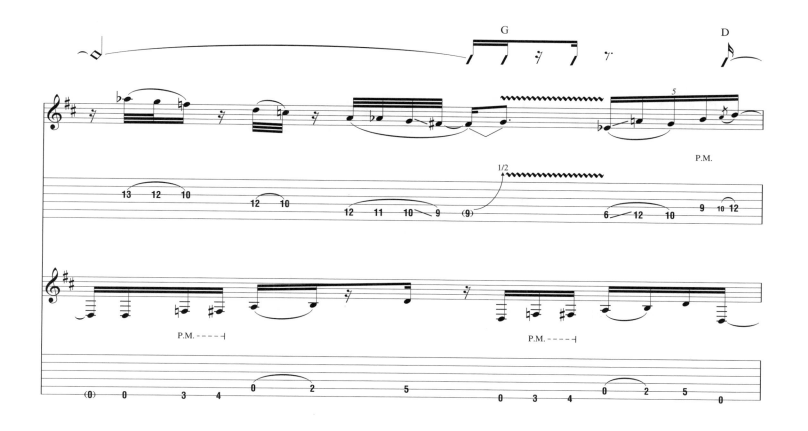

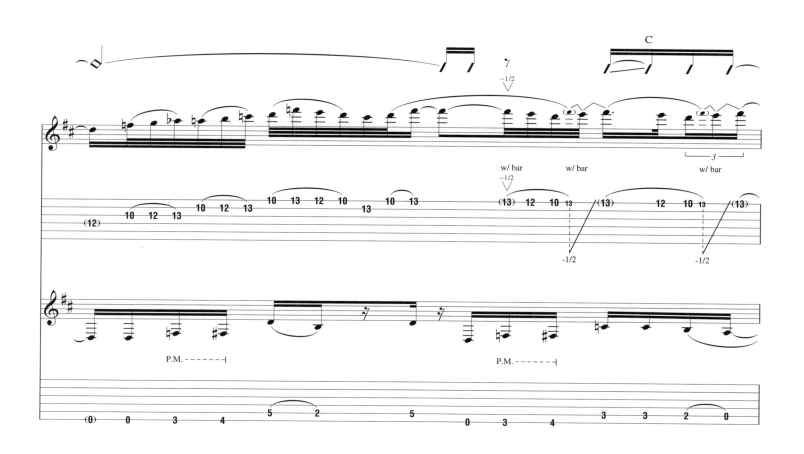

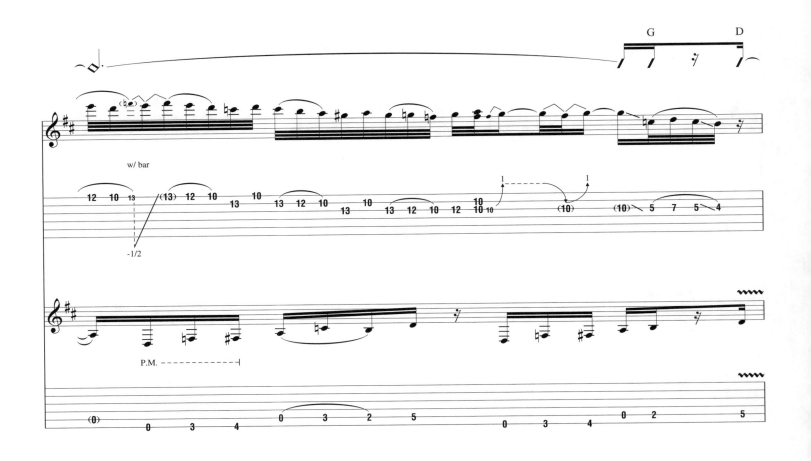

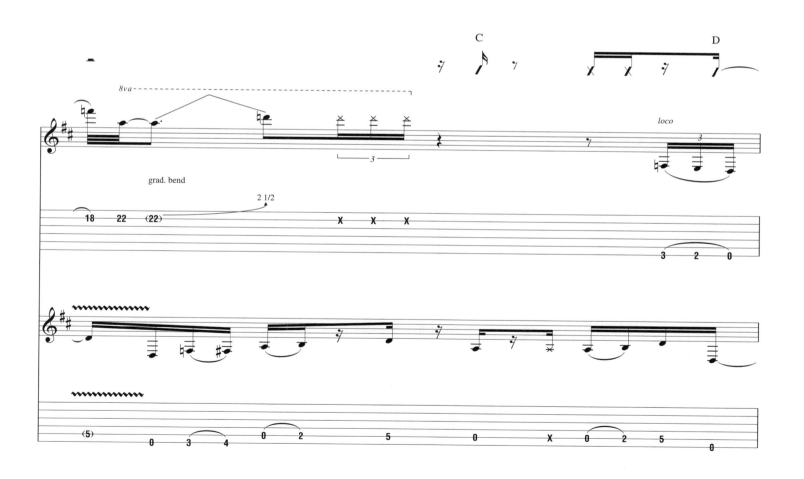

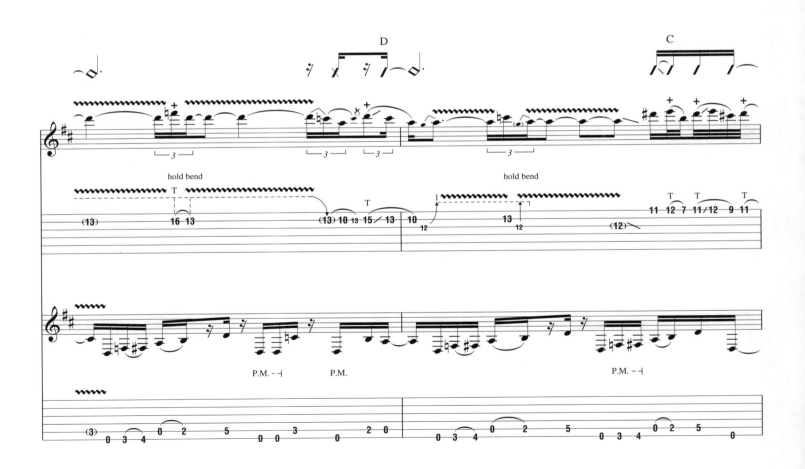

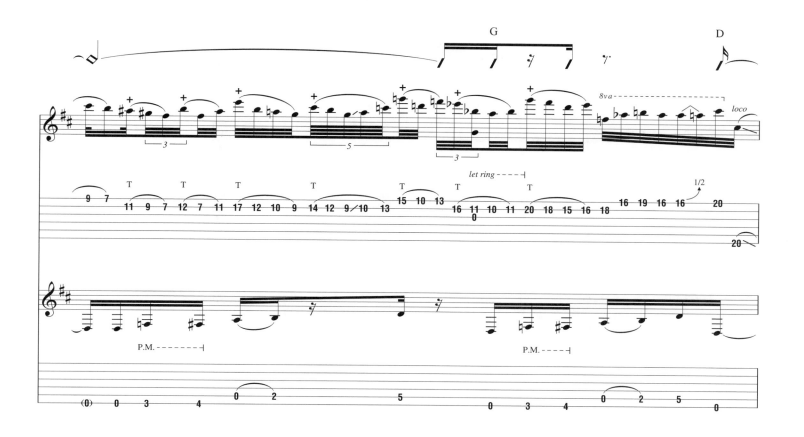

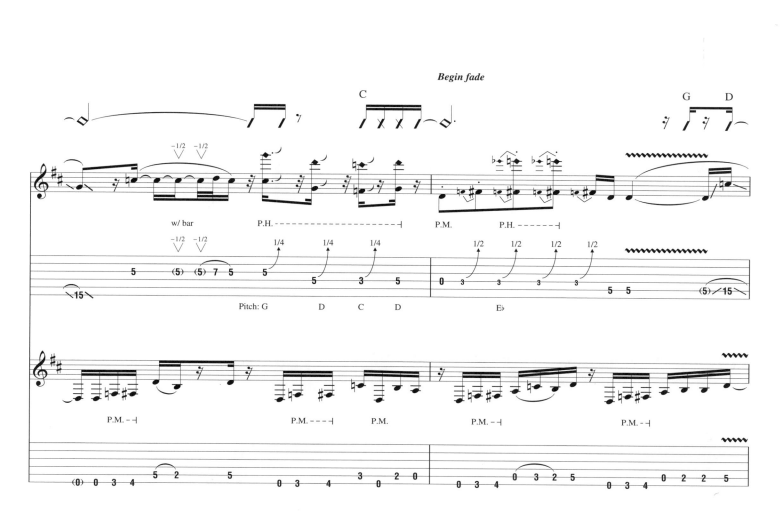

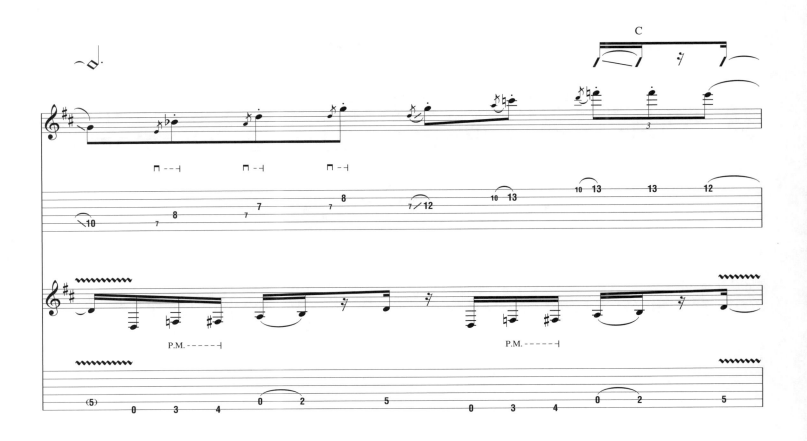

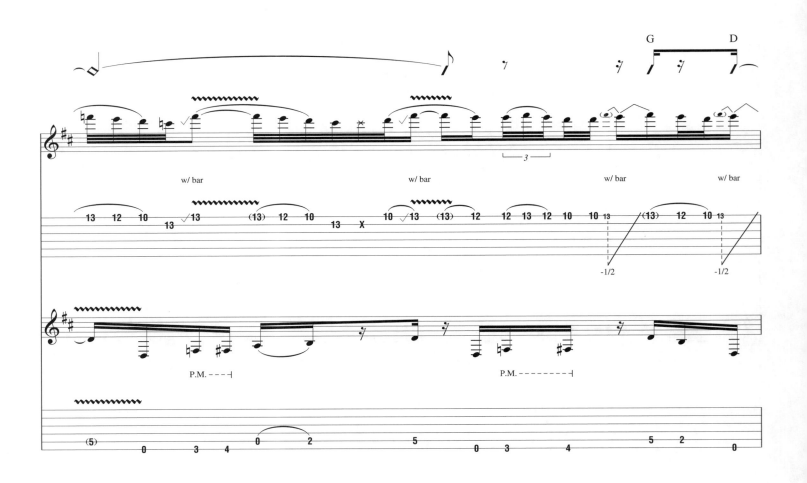

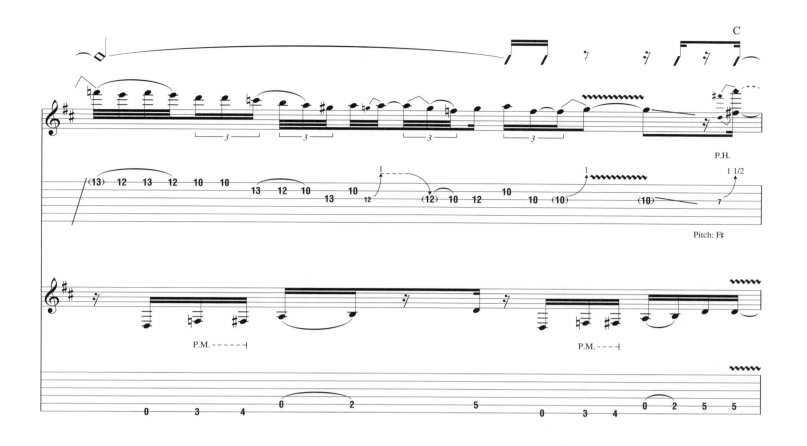

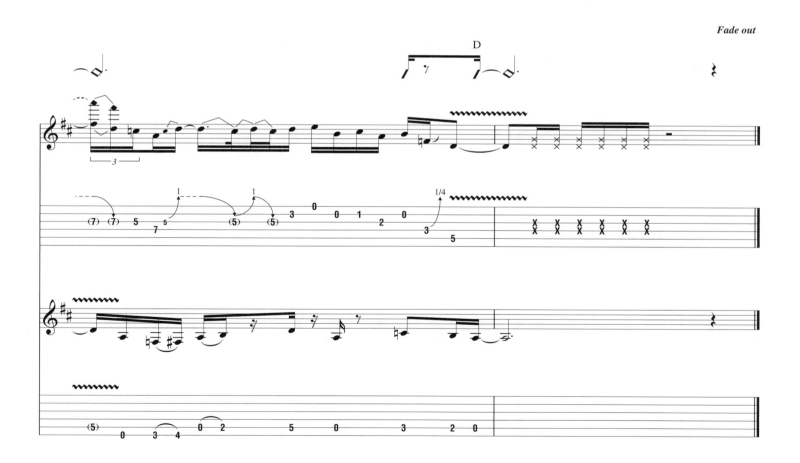

from *Van Halen*

Eruption

Music by David Lee Roth, Edward Van Halen, Alex Van Halen and Michael Anthony

Tune down 1/2 step:
(low to high) Eb-Ab-Db-Gb-Bb-Eb

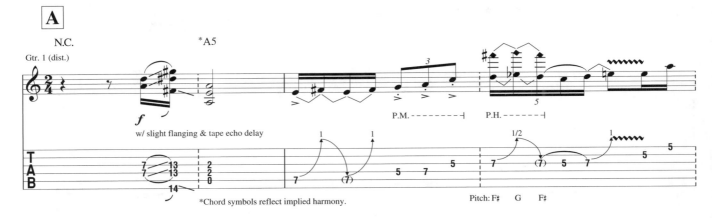

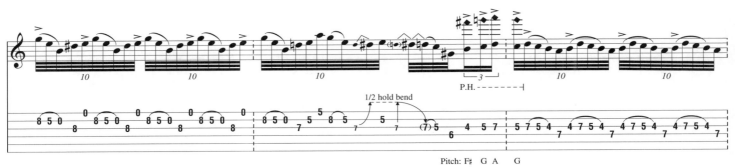

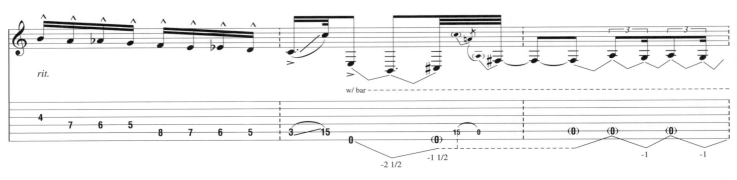

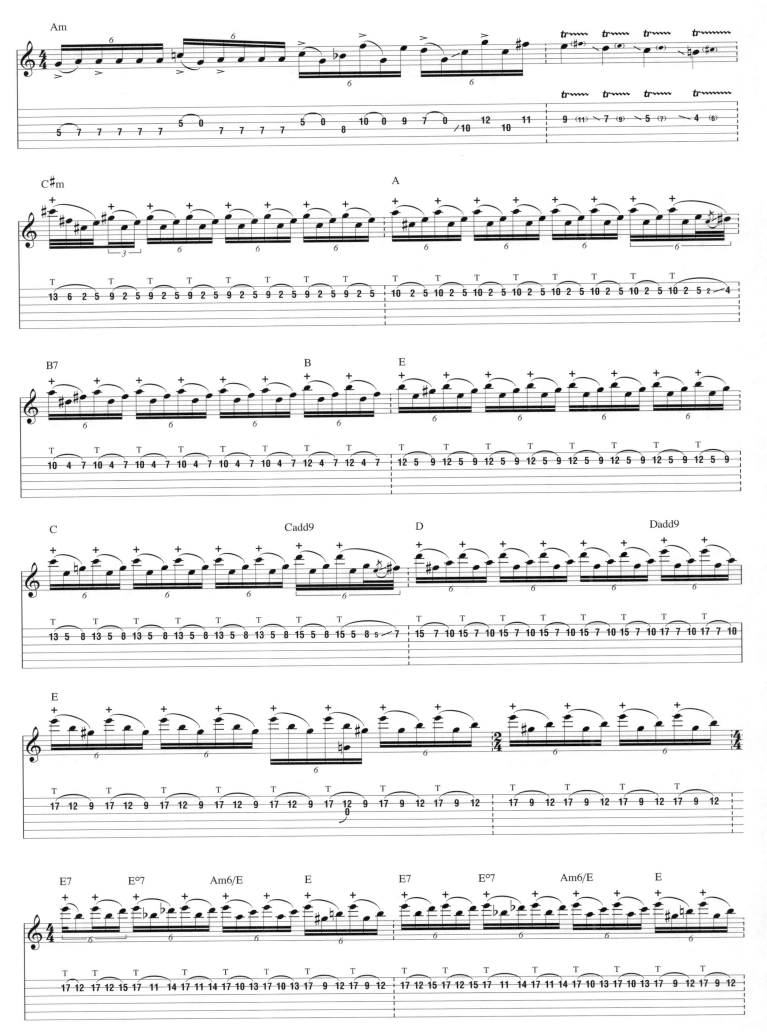

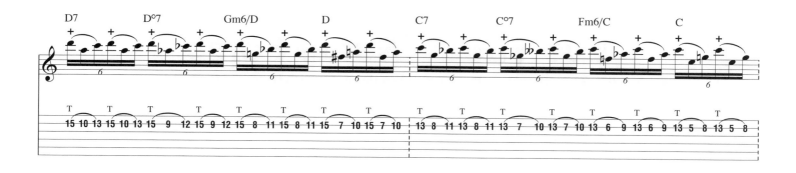

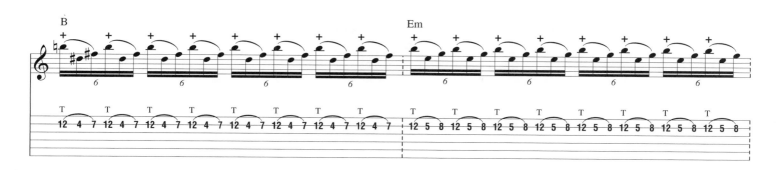

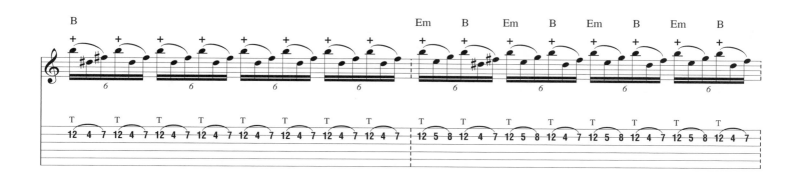

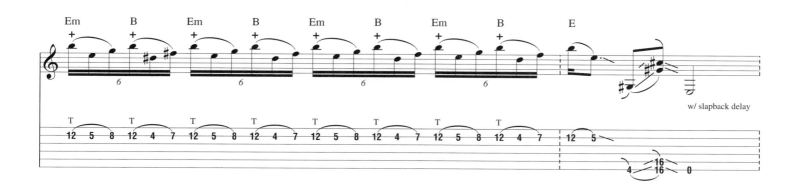

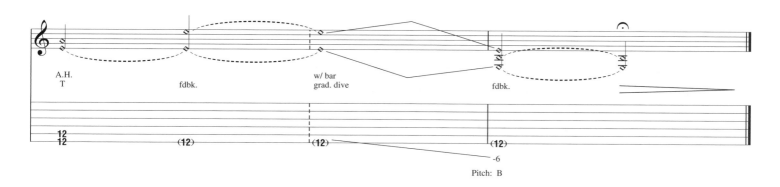

from *Women and Children First*

Everybody Wants Some

Words and Music by David Lee Roth, Edward Van Halen, Alex Van Halen and Michael Anthony

Tune down 1/2 step:
(low to high) Eb-Ab-Db-Gb-Bb-Eb

Intro
Moderately ♩ = 142

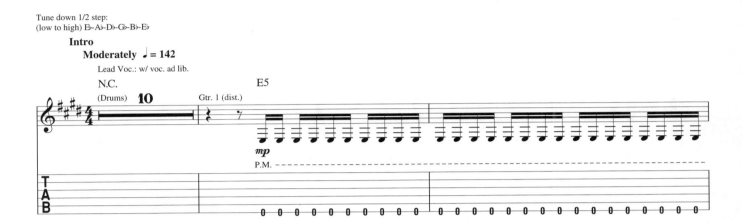

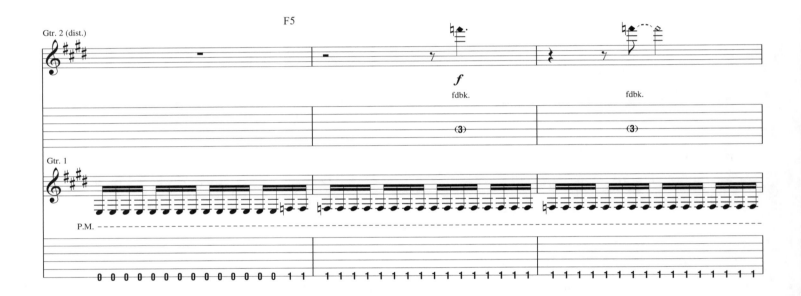

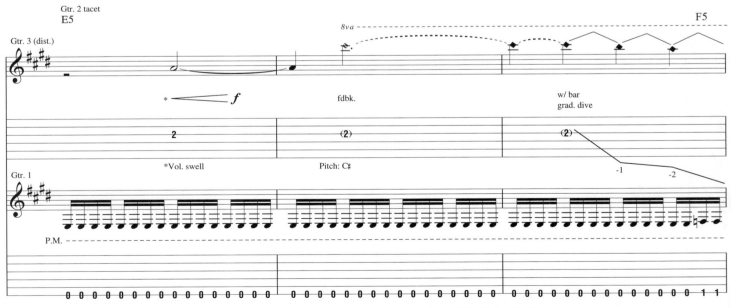

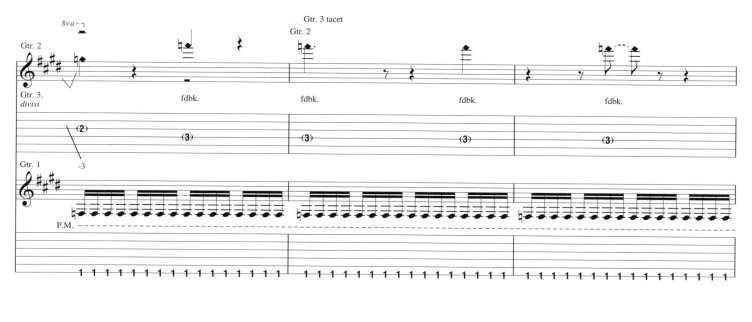

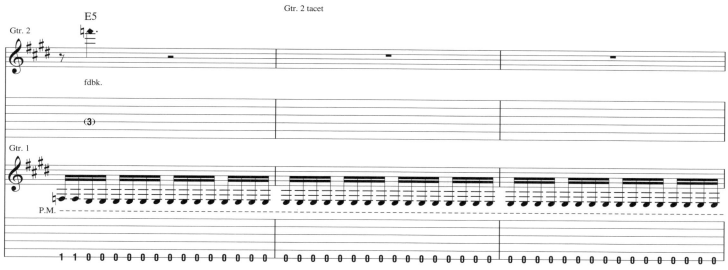

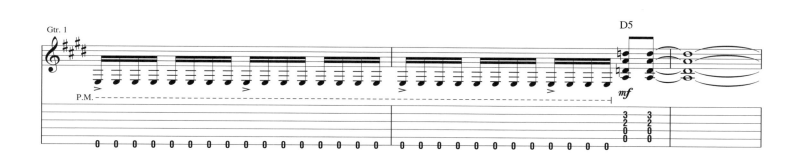

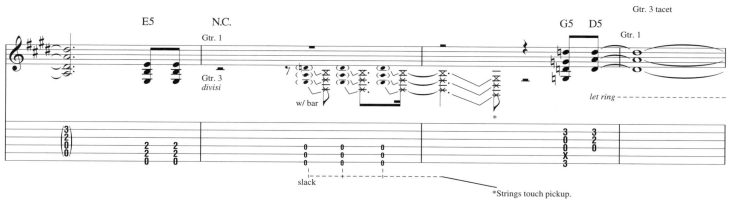

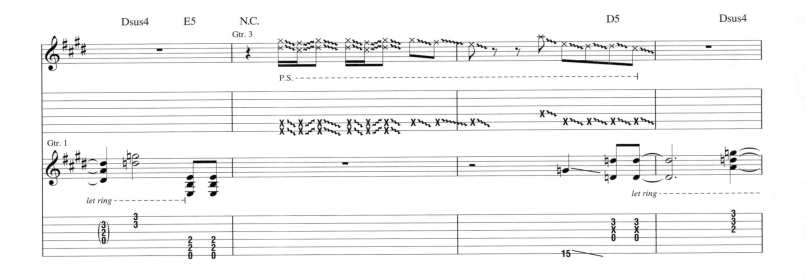

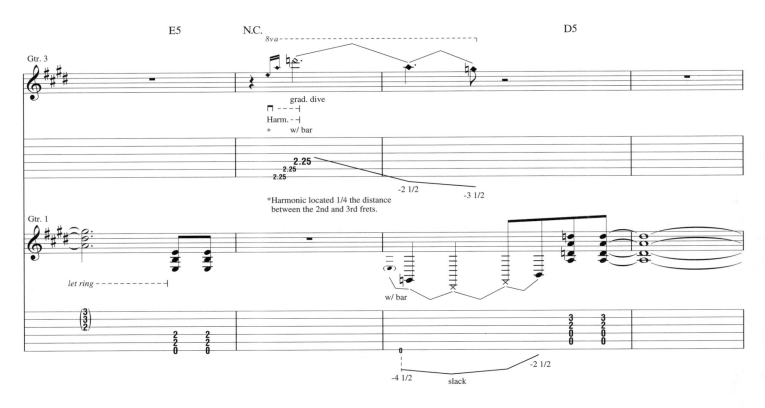

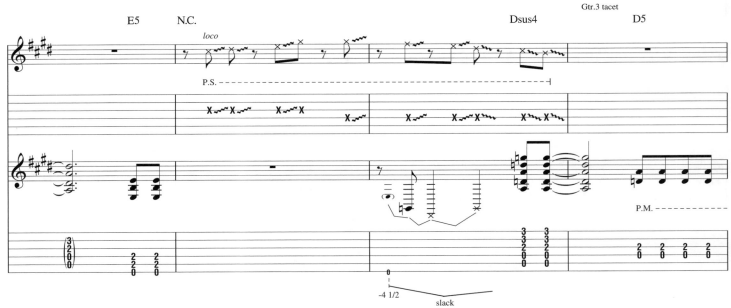

Interlude

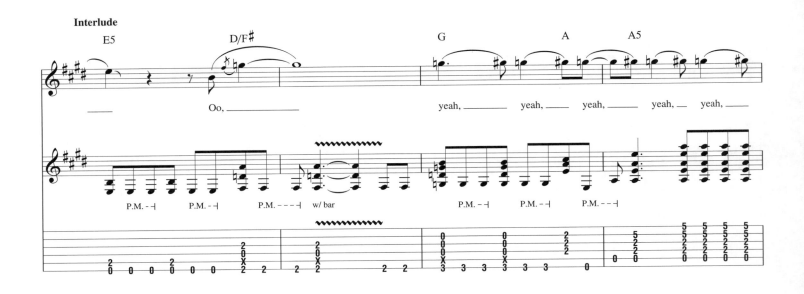

Guitar Solo

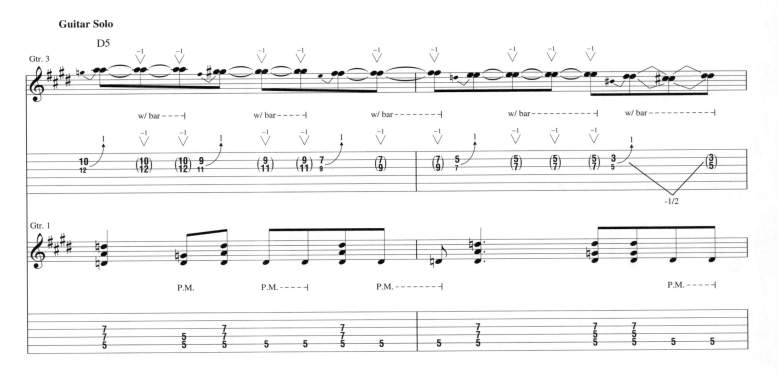

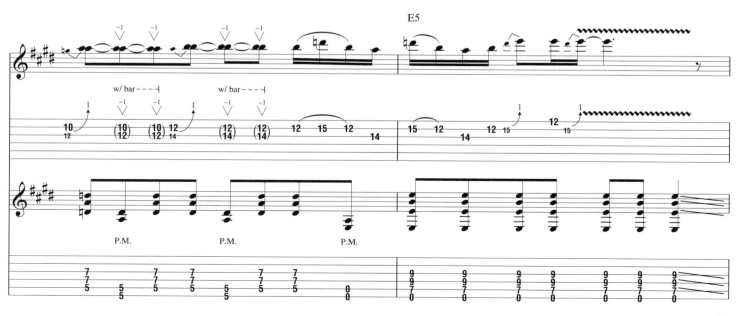

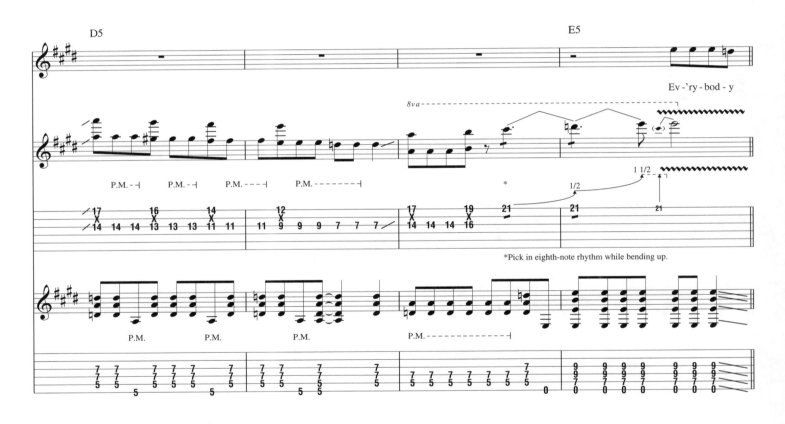

Chorus

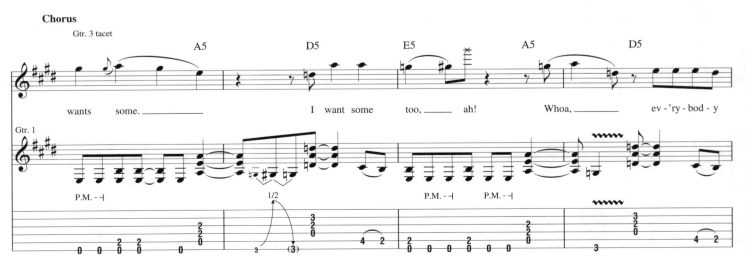

Interlude

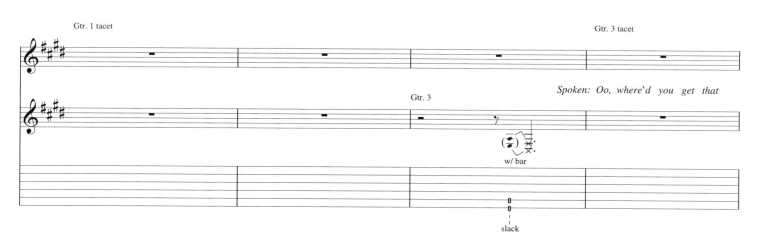

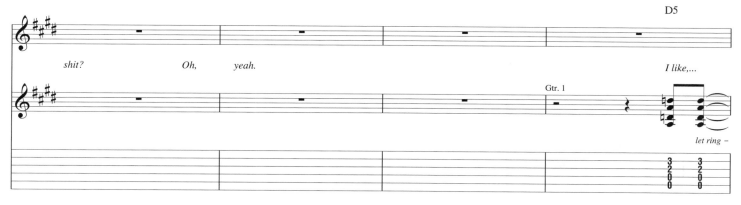

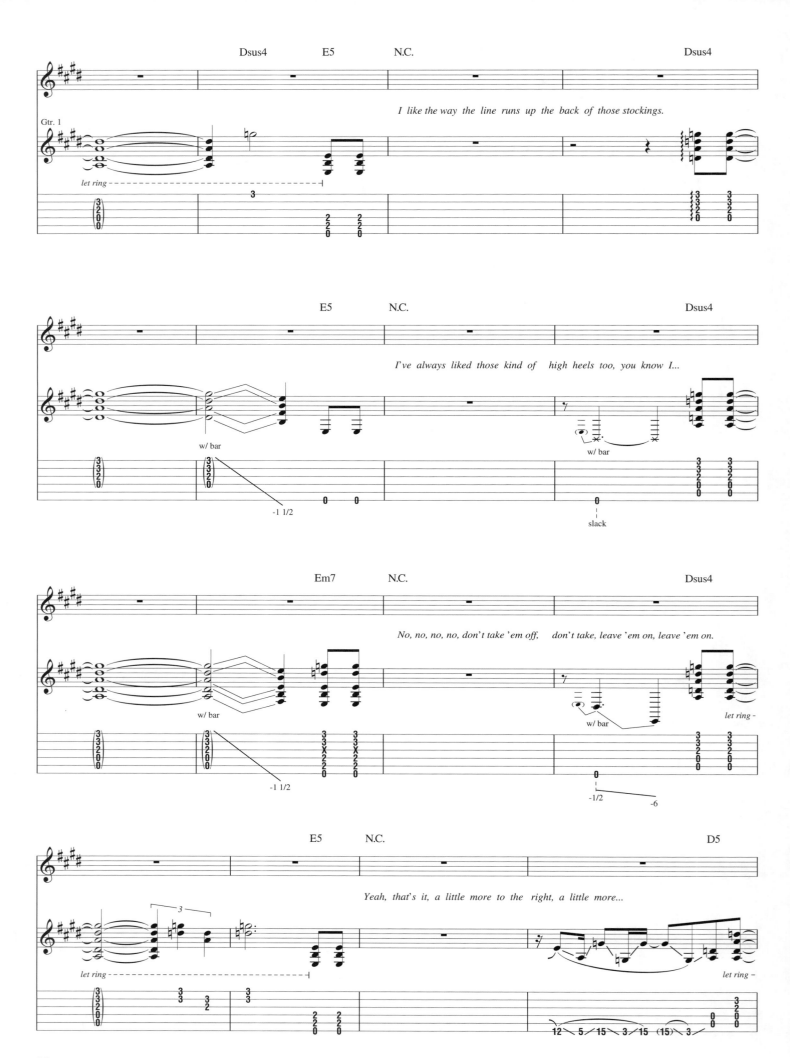

I like the way the line runs up the back of those stockings.

I've always liked those kind of high heels too, you know I...

No, no, no, no, don't take 'em off, don't take, leave 'em on, leave 'em on.

Yeah, that's it, a little more to the right, a little more...

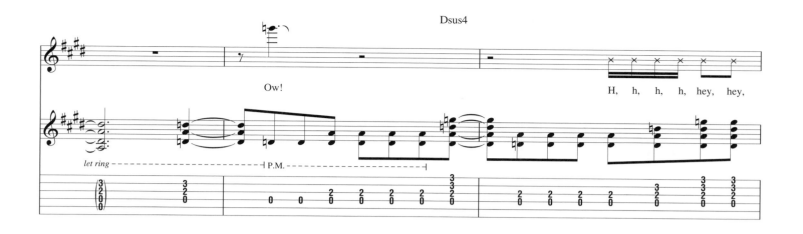

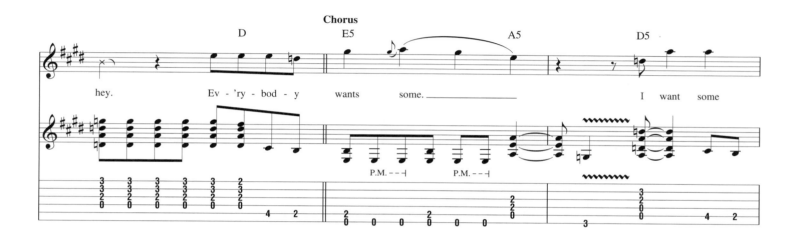

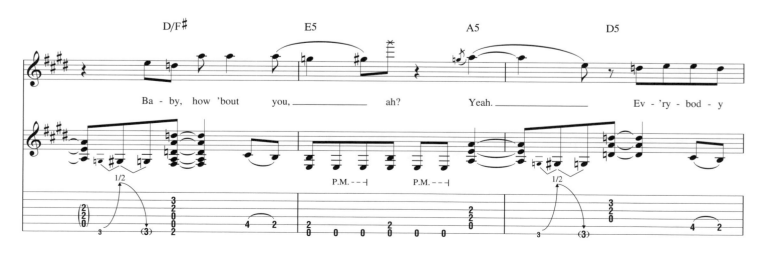

Outro

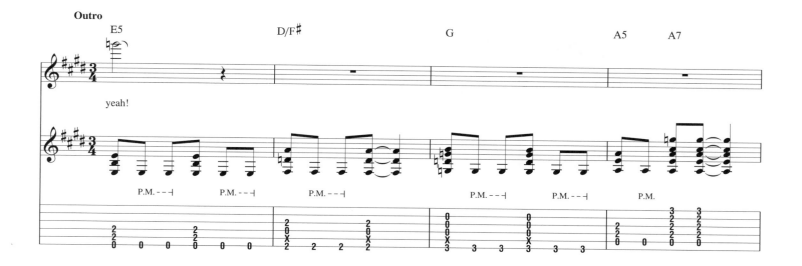

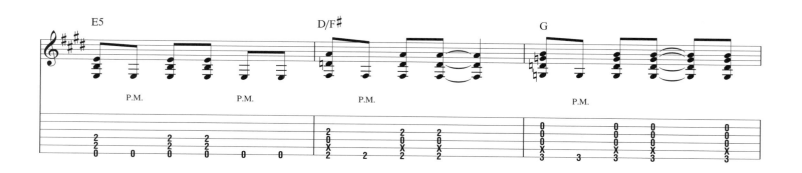

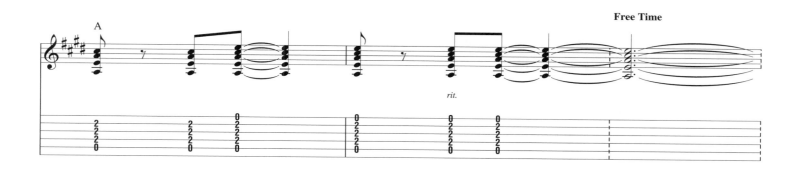

Free Time

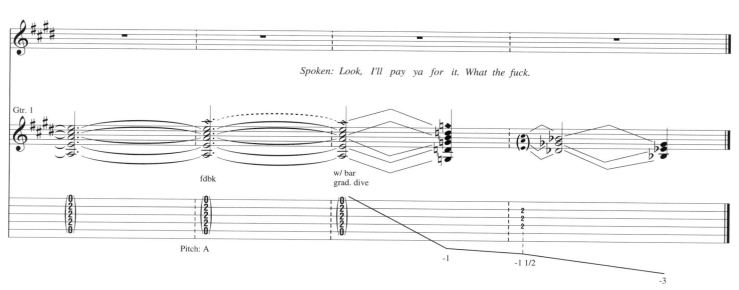

Spoken: Look, I'll pay ya for it. What the fuck.

Feel Your Love Tonight

Words and Music by David Lee Roth, Edward Van Halen, Alex Van Halen and Michael Anthony

Tune down 1/2 step:
(low to high) E♭-A♭-D♭-G♭-B♭-E♭

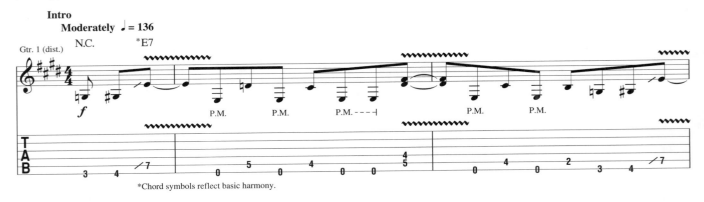

*Chord symbols reflect basic harmony.

Al - right!

Verse

1. We're get - tin' fun - ny in the back of my car.

Rhy. Fig. 1

Gtr. 1: w/ Rhy. Fig. 2

bet - ter use it up be - fore it gets old, __ no. I tell you, hon - ey, now you've let your life grow cold, __

__ no. Uh, no, no, no. _____ I'm a beg - gin', uh, you. __

Bkgd. Vocs.: w/ Voc. Fig. 1

__ I'm on __ my knees. __ I __

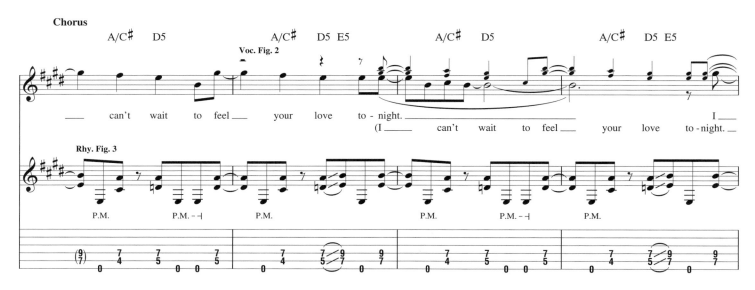

Chorus

__ can't wait to feel __ your love to - night. I __
(I __ can't wait to feel __ your love to - night. __

Verse

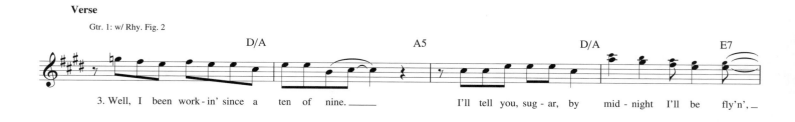

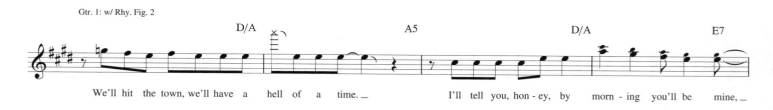

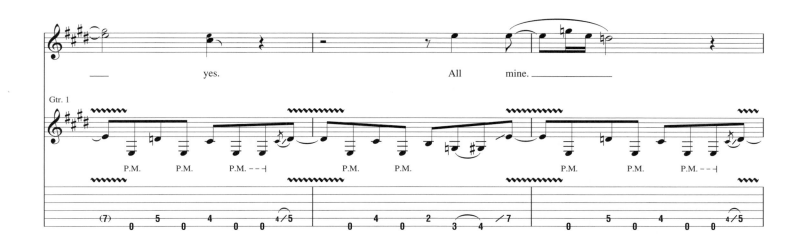

yes.   All mine. _____

Bkgd. Vocs.: w/ Voc. Fig. 1

C(#11)   C   F#5   B5

You know I'm beg-gin' you, ba - by.   I'm on my knees. _____

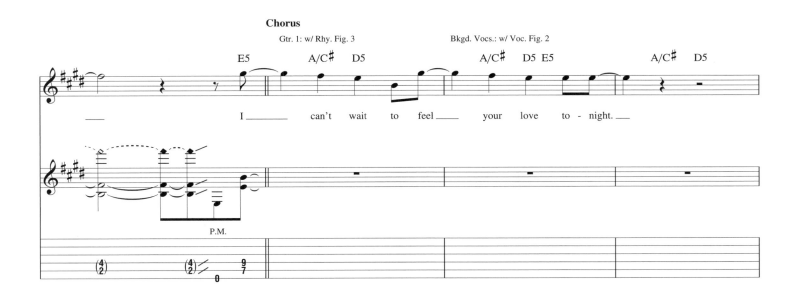

Chorus

Gtr. 1: w/ Rhy. Fig. 3   Bkgd. Vocs.: w/ Voc. Fig. 2

E5   A/C#   D5   A/C#   D5 E5   A/C#   D5

_____ I _____ can't wait to feel _____ your love to - night. _____

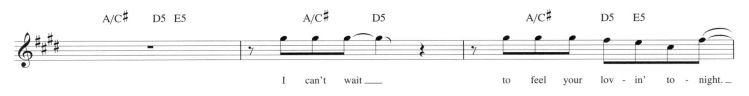

A/C#   D5 E5   A/C#   D5   A/C#   D5 E5

I   can't wait _____   to feel your lov - in' to - night.

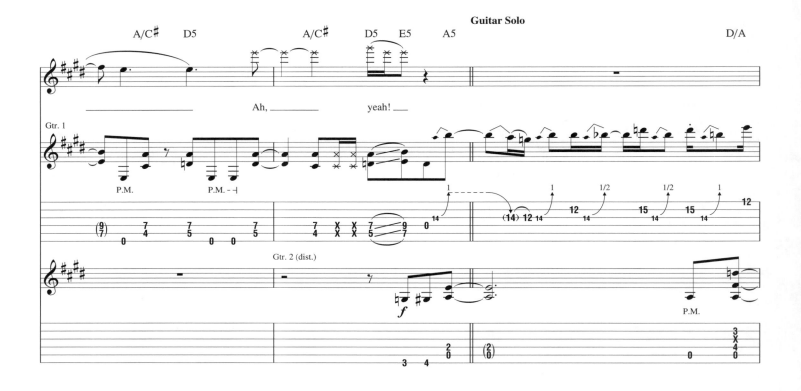

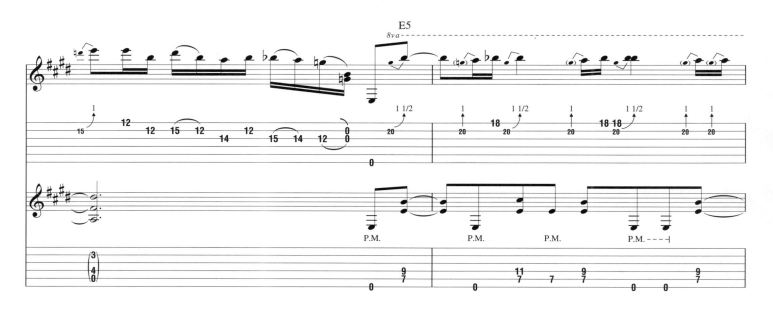

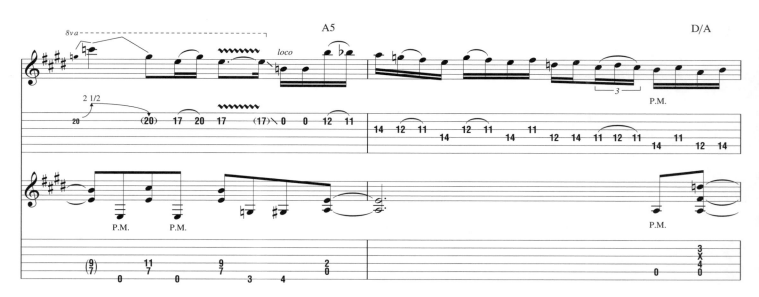

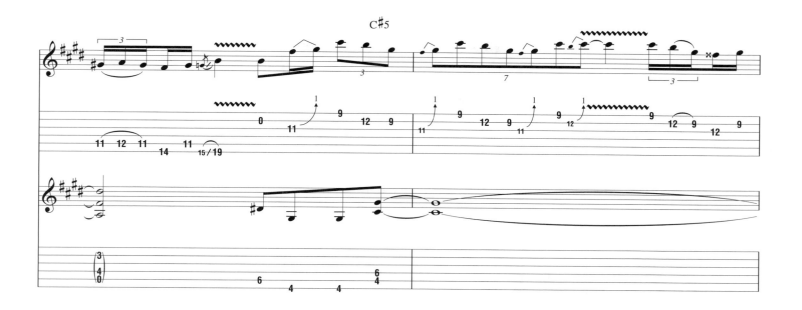

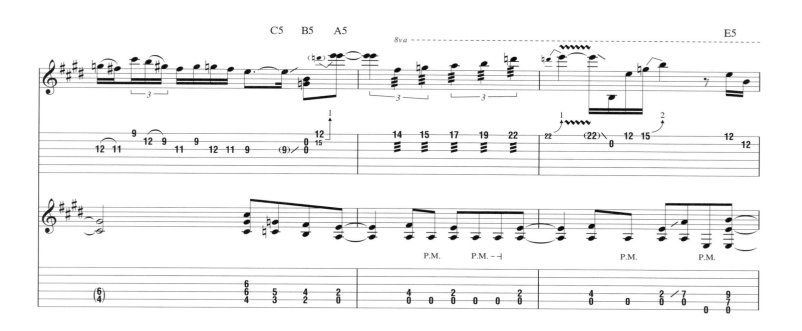

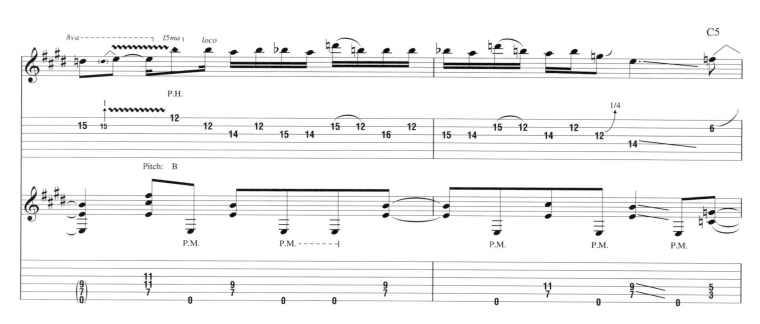

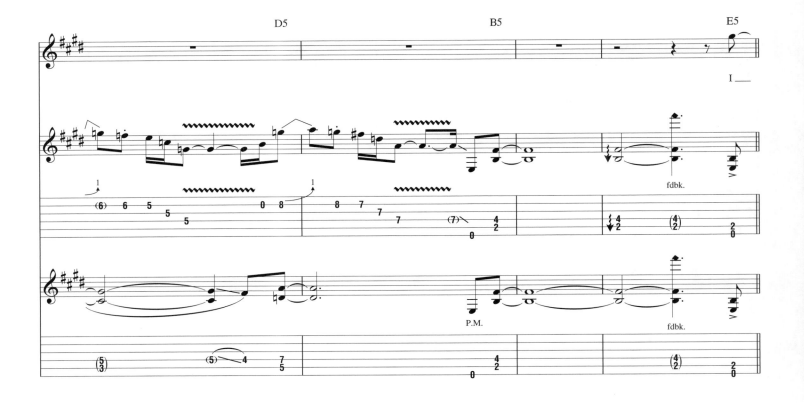

Outro-Chorus

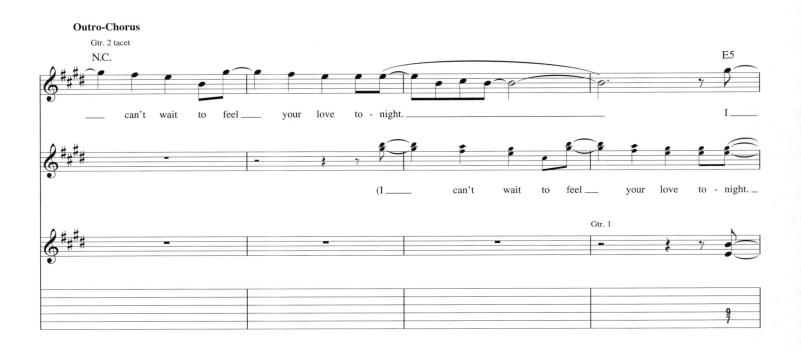

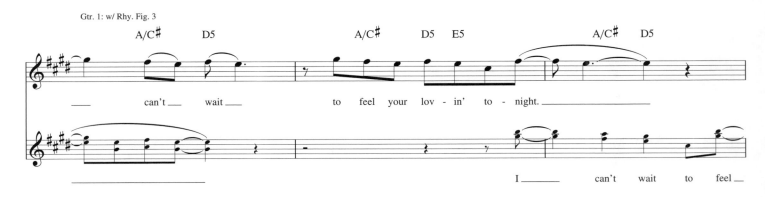

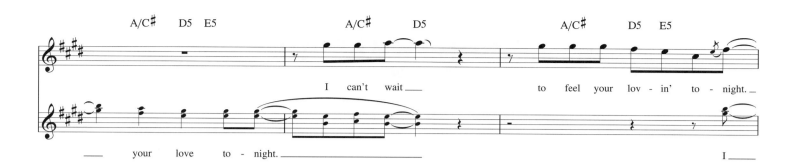

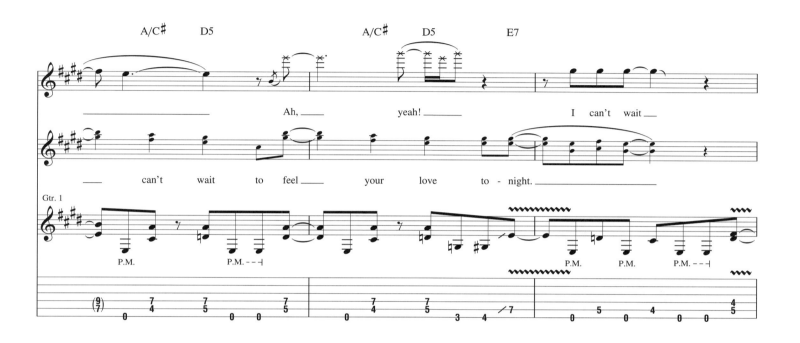

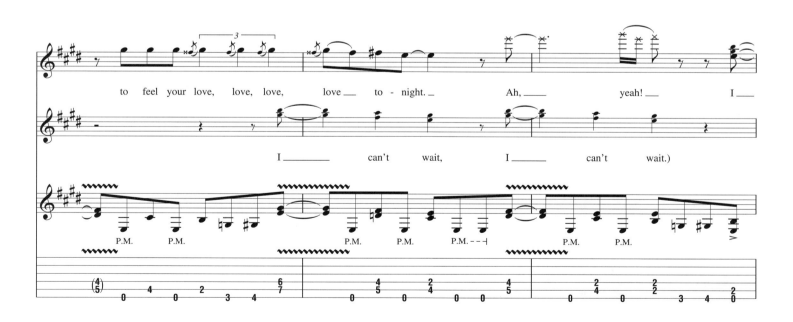

from *Diver Down*

Hang 'Em High

Words and Music by David Lee Roth, Edward Van Halen, Alex Van Halen and Michael Anthony

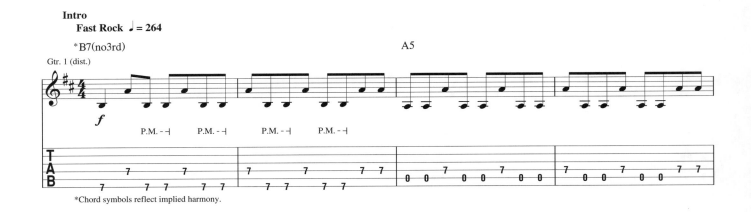

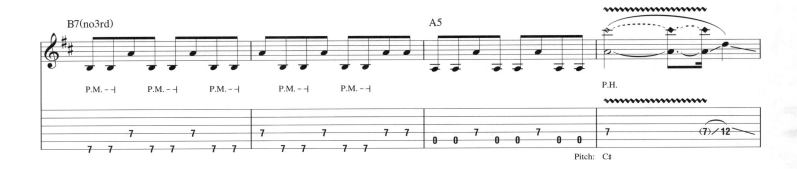

*Chord symbols reflect implied harmony.

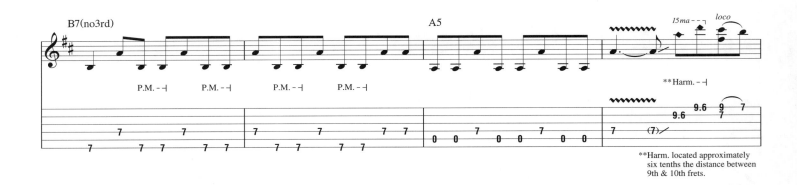

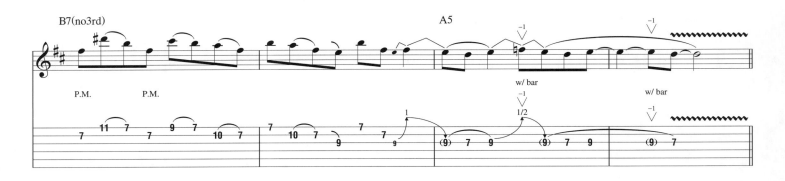

Verse

*Vocals doubled next 16 meas.

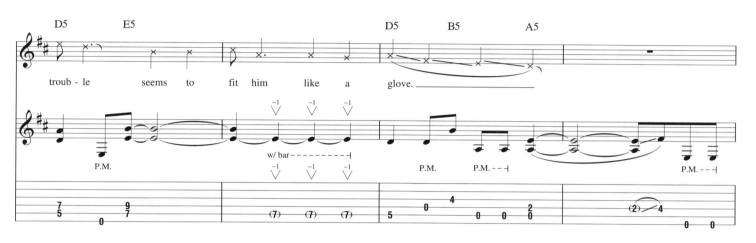

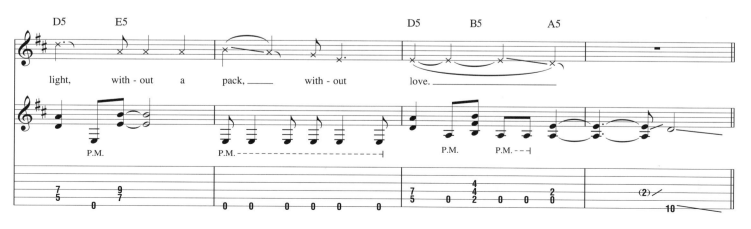

Chorus

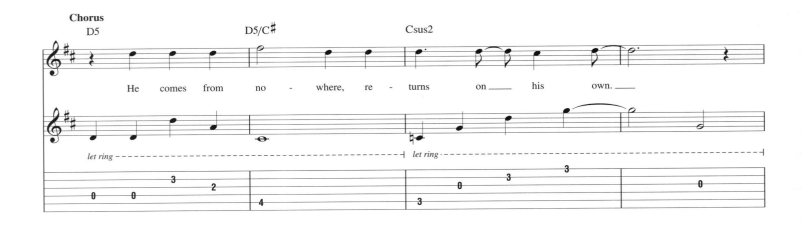

He comes from no - where, re - turns on ___ his own. ___

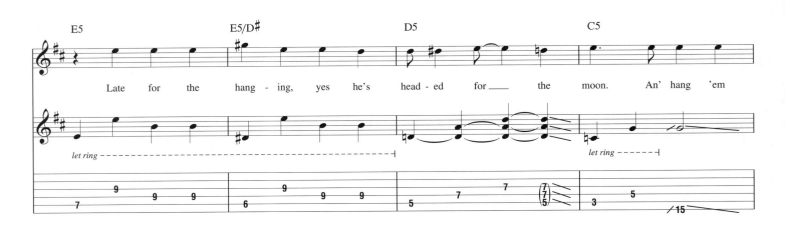

Late for the hang - ing, yes he's head - ed for ___ the moon. An' hang 'em

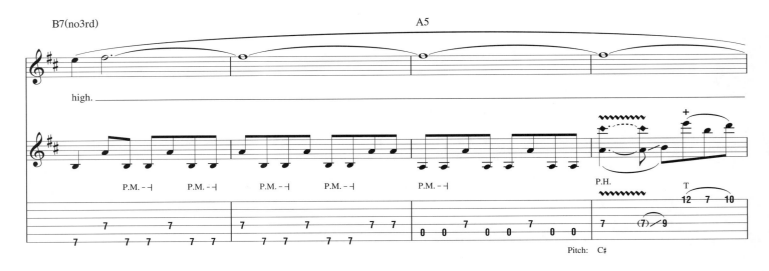

high. ___

Pitch: C♯

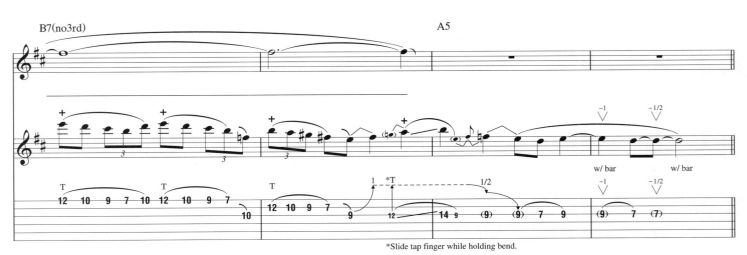

*Slide tap finger while holding bend.

Verse

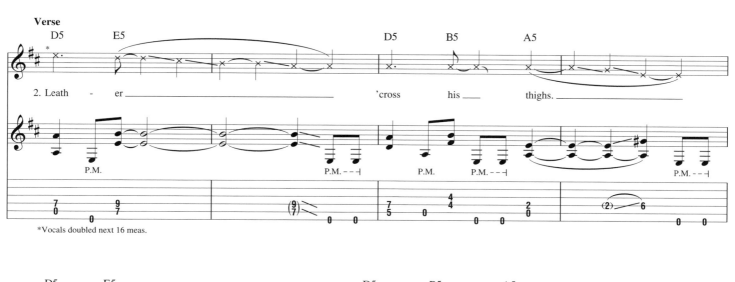

2. Leath - er _____ 'cross his ___ thighs. _____

*Vocals doubled next 16 meas.

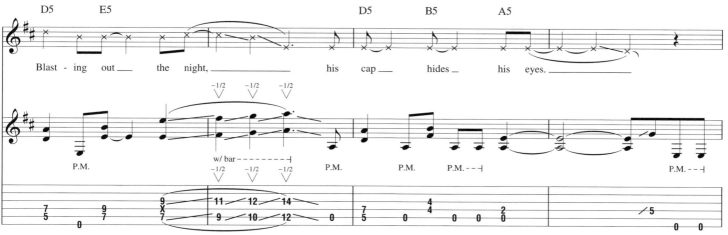

Blast - ing out ___ the night, _____ his cap ___ hides ___ his eyes. _____

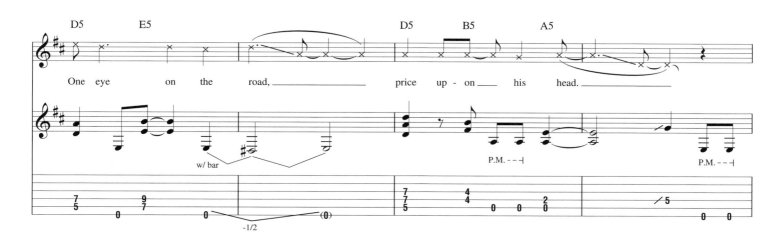

One eye on the road, _____ price up - on ___ his head. _____

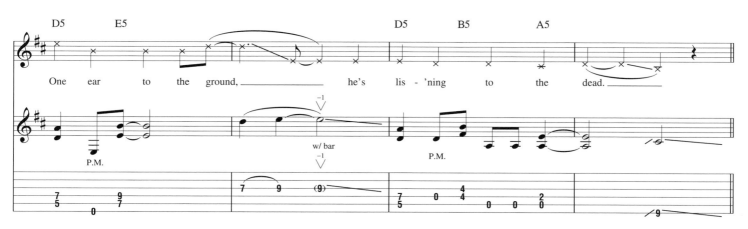

One ear to the ground, _____ he's lis - 'ning to the dead. _____

Chorus

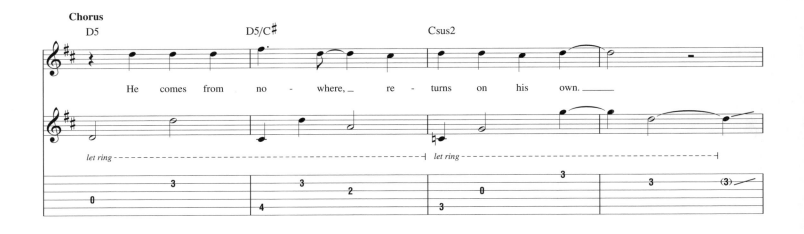

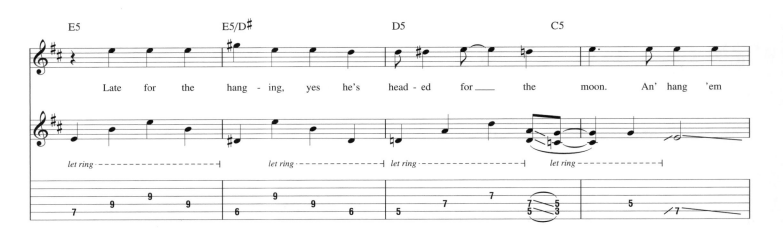

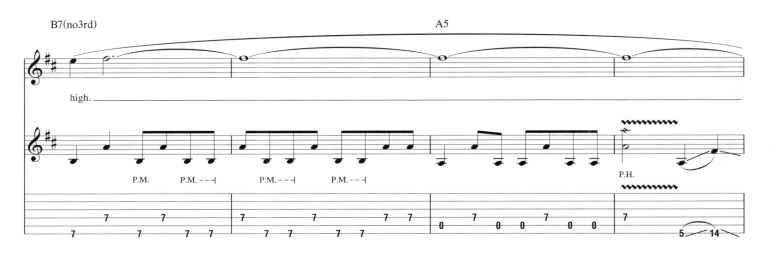

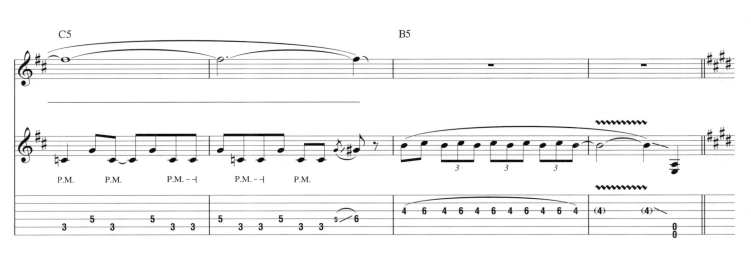

Guitar Solo

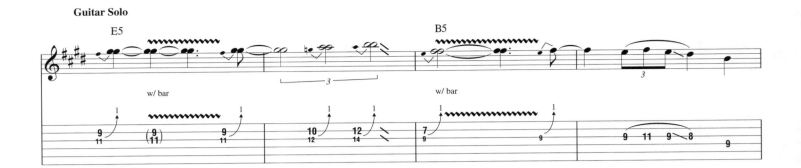

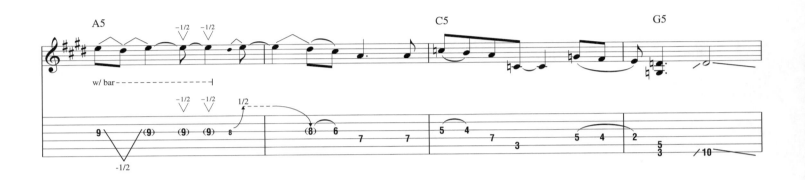

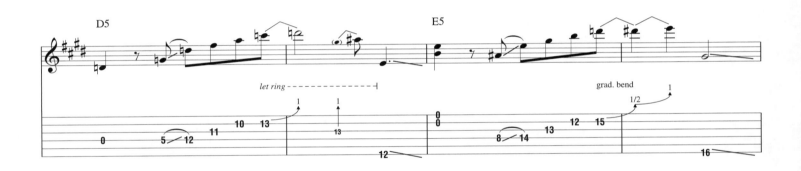

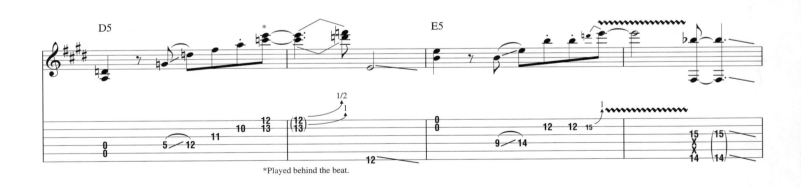

*Played behind the beat.

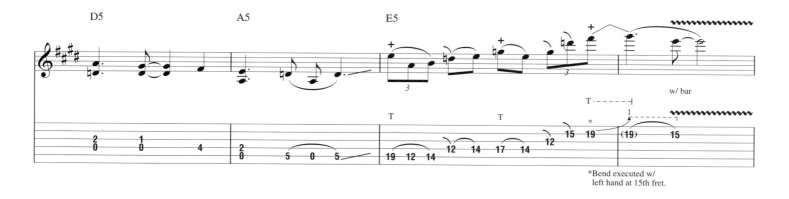

*Bend executed w/
left hand at 15th fret.

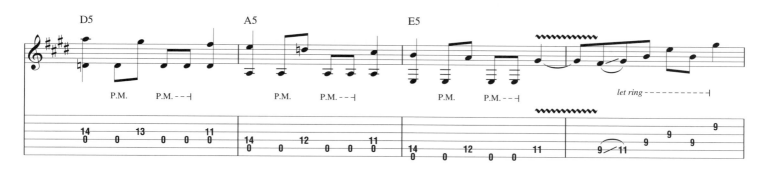

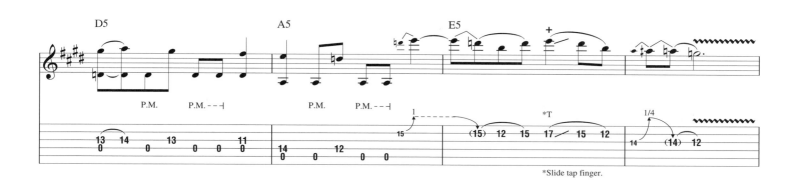

*Slide tap finger.

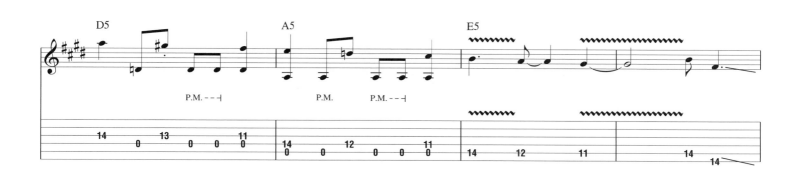

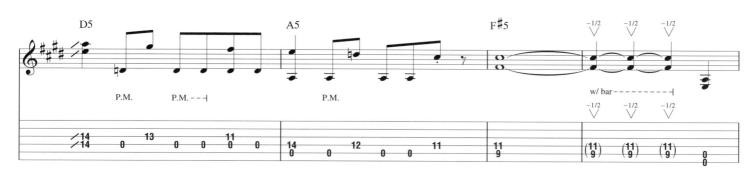

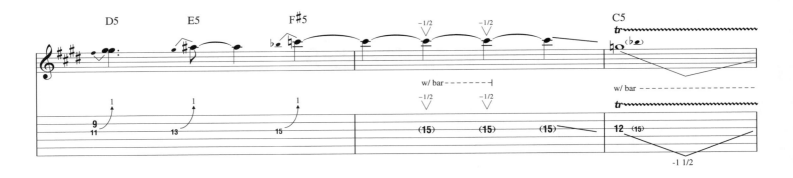

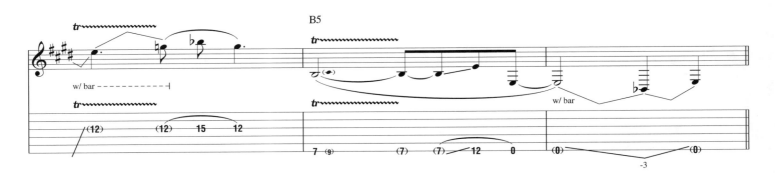

Bridge

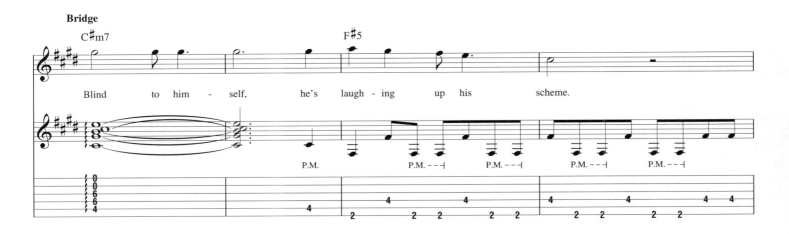

Blind to him-self, he's laugh-ing up his scheme.

Gtr. 1: w/ Rhy. Fig. 1

Look-ing back in an - ger, the cit - y is __ re - lieved. __ Vi - sion of light,

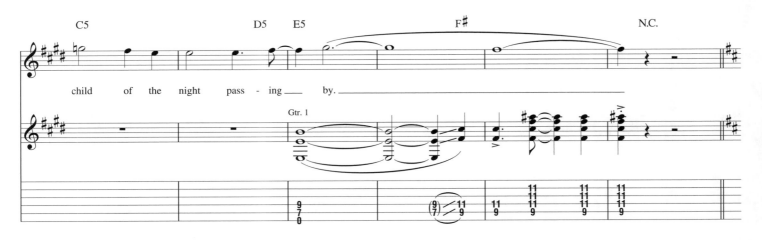

child of the night pass - ing __ by. _____

Interlude

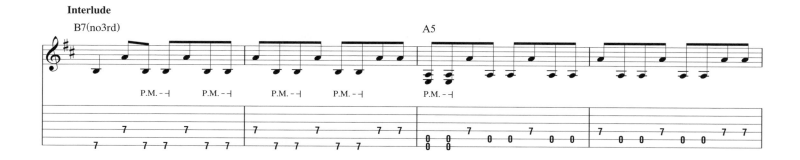

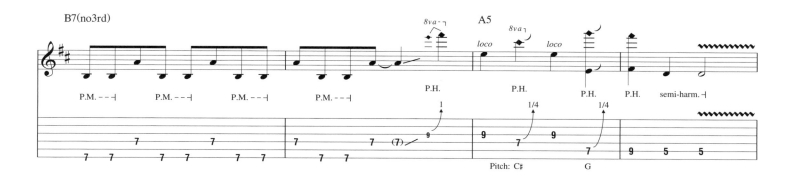

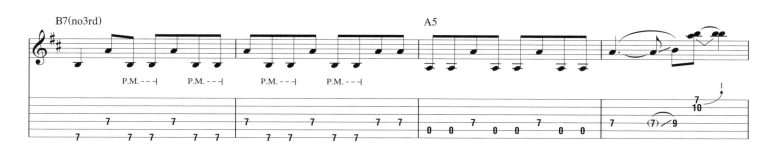

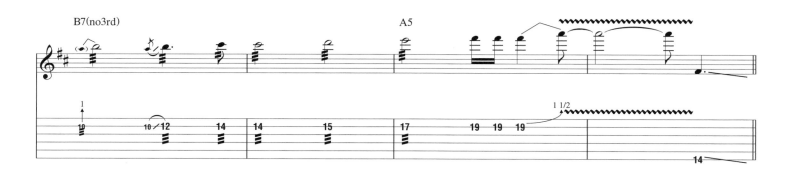

Verse

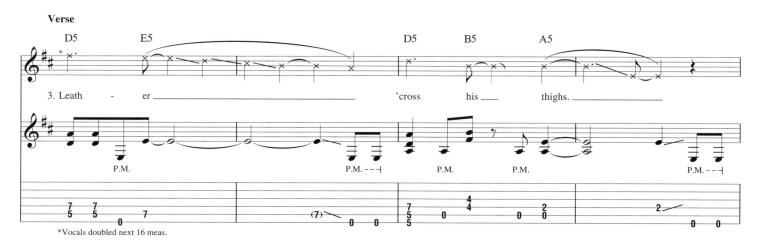

3. Leath - er _____ 'cross his ___ thighs. _____

*Vocals doubled next 16 meas.

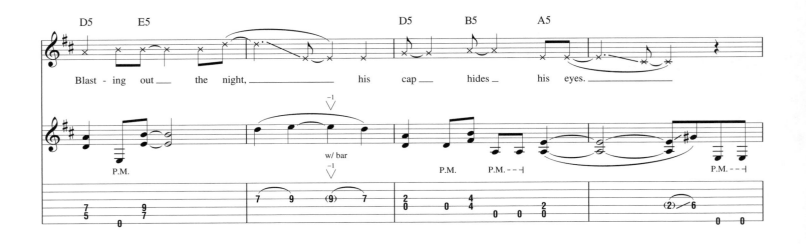

Blast-ing out ___ the night, _____ his cap ___ hides ___ his eyes. _____

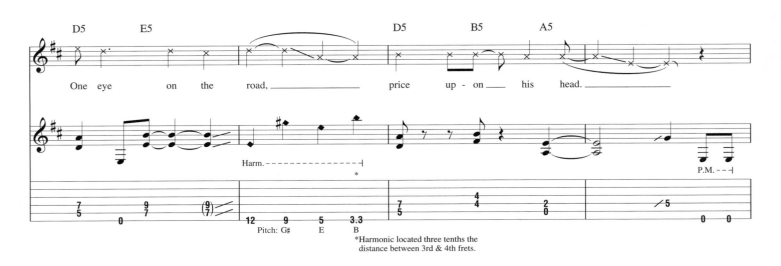

One eye ___ on the road, _____ price up-on ___ his head. _____

*Harmonic located three tenths the
distance between 3rd & 4th frets.

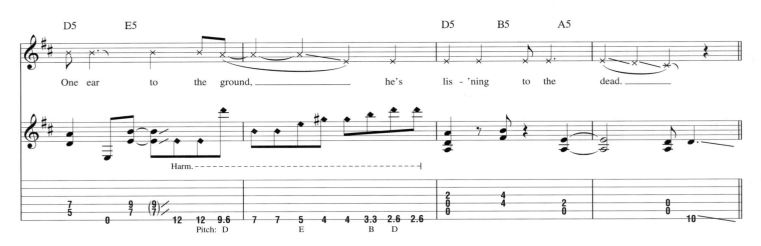

One ear ___ to the ground, _____ he's lis-'ning to the dead. _____

Chorus

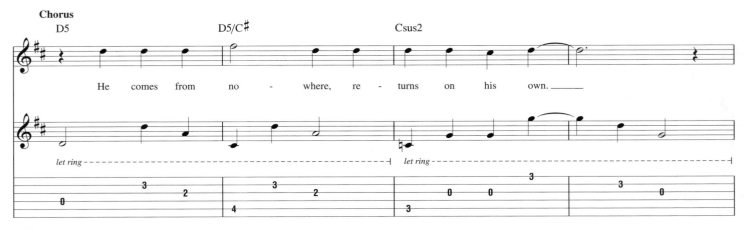

He comes from no - where, re - turns on his own. ___

114

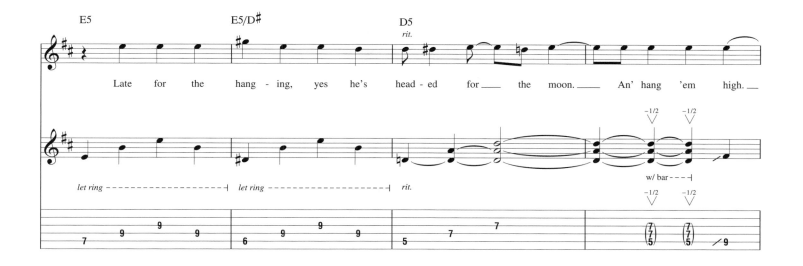

Late for the hang - ing, yes he's head - ed for ___ the moon. ___ An' hang 'em high. ___

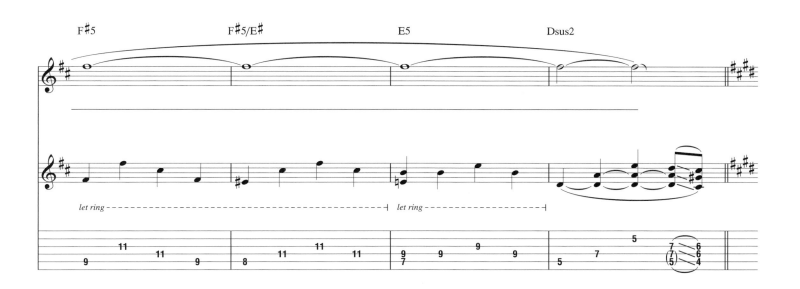

Outro
Free time

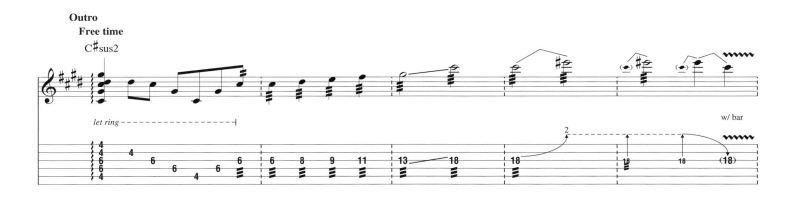

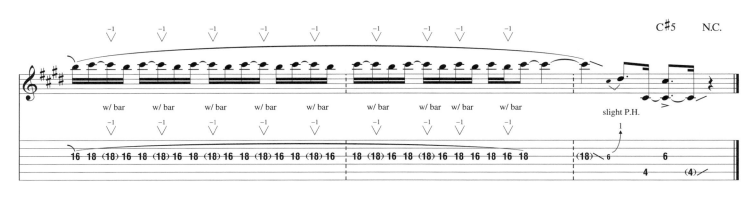

from *Van Halen*

Jamie's Cryin'

Words and Music by David Lee Roth, Edward Van Halen, Alex Van Halen and Michael Anthony

Tune down 1/2 step:
(low to high) E♭-A♭-D♭-G♭-B♭-E♭

*Composite arrangement

**Chord symbols reflect implied harmony.

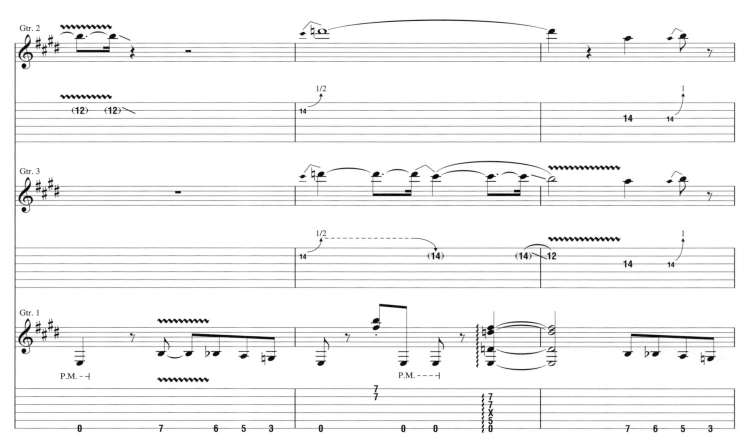

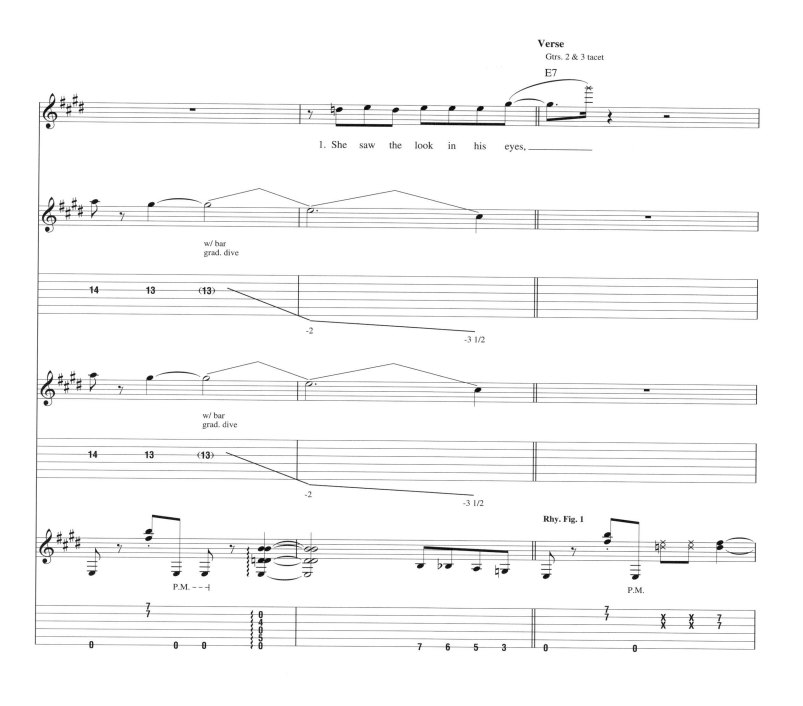

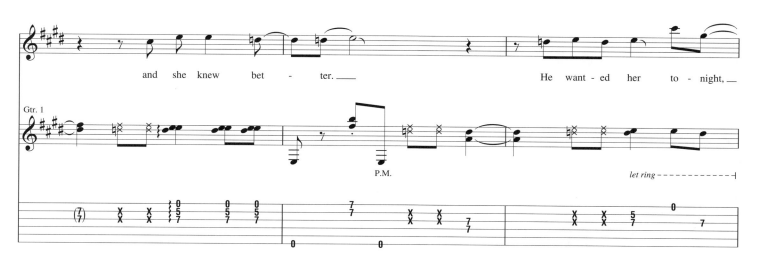

cry - in'.   2. Now, Ja - mie would-n't   say, "Al - right," ah!

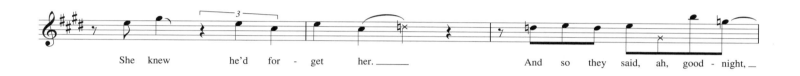

She knew   he'd for - get her. _____   And so they said, ah, good - night, _

_ ah.   Oh, _ and now he's gone for - ev - er.   She wants to send him a let -

Pre-Chorus

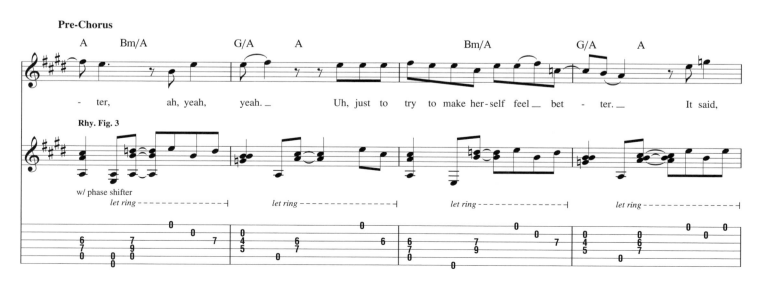

- ter,   ah, yeah,   yeah. _   Uh, just to try to make her-self feel _ bet - ter. _   It said,

"Gim-me..." But she knows _____ what that-'ll get her. _____
("Gim-me a call _____ some - time.") _____

Chorus

Oh, whoa, whoa, Ja - mie's cry - in'.

Oh, whoa, whoa, Ja - mie's cry - in'. Now, Ja - mie's been in love _____ be -

Bridge

fore _____ and she knows what love is for. It should mean _____ a lit-tle, a lit-tle
(Ah, _____ ah, _____

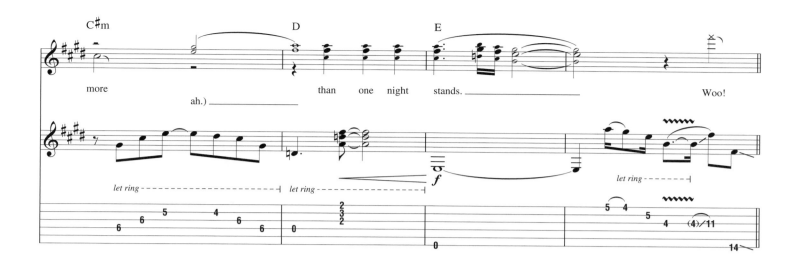

more ah.) than one night stands. Woo!

Guitar Solo

slight P.H. P.M. P.M.

She wants to send him a let-

Pre-Chorus

Gtr. 1: w/ Rhy. Fig. 3

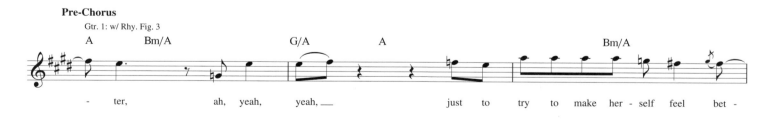

-ter, ah, yeah, yeah, just to try to make her-self feel bet-

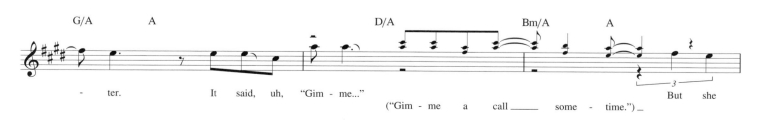

-ter. It said, uh, "Gim - me..." But she
("Gim - me a call some - time.")

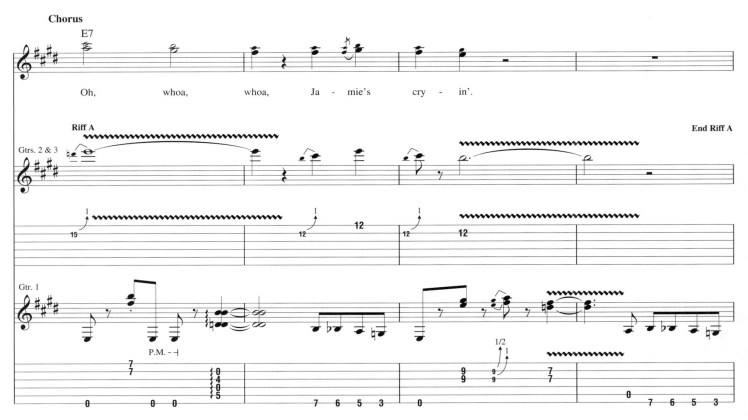

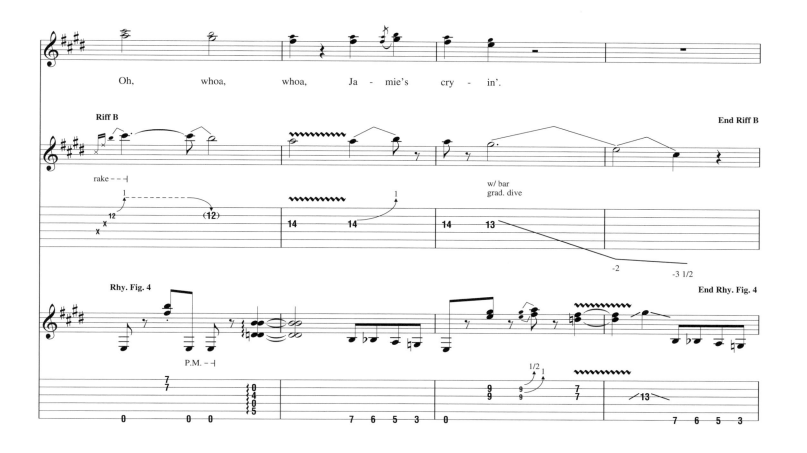

Oh, whoa, whoa, Ja - mie's cry - in'.

Gtr. 1: w/ Rhy. Fig. 4 (2 times)
Gtrs. 2 & 3: w/ Riff A

Oh, whoa, whoa, Ja - mie's cry - in'.

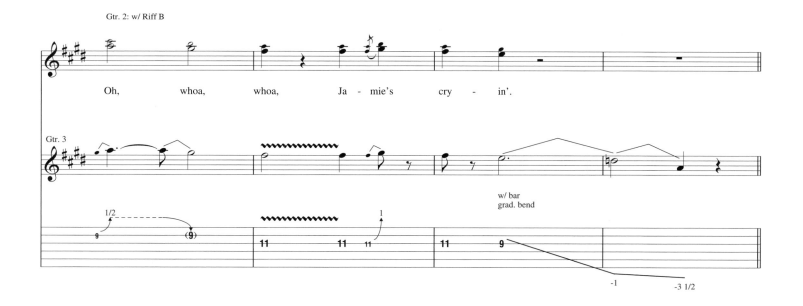

Gtr. 2: w/ Riff B

Oh, whoa, whoa, Ja - mie's cry - in'.

Outro

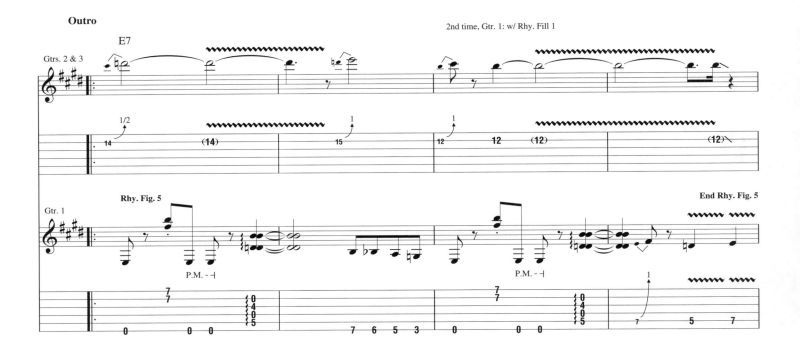

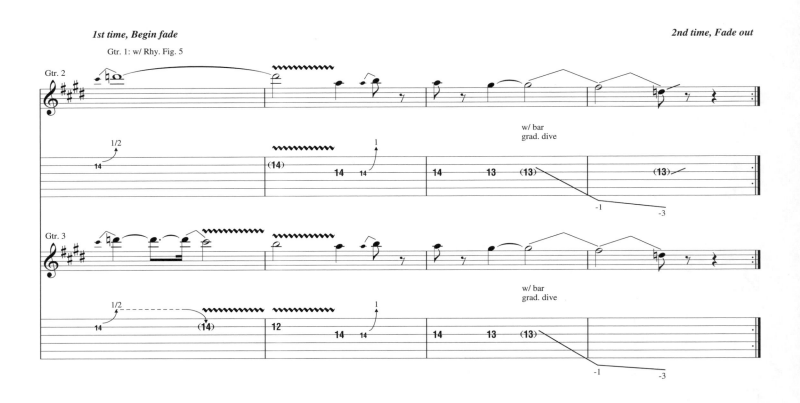

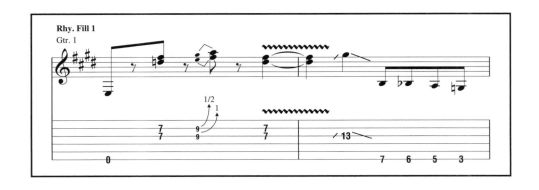

from *1984*

Jump

Words and Music by David Lee Roth, Edward Van Halen, Alex Van Halen and Michael Anthony

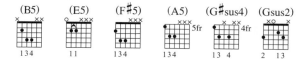

Gtrs. 2, 3, & 4: Tune up 1/2 step:
(low to high) E♯-A♯-D♯-G♯-B♯-E♯

Intro
Moderately ♩ = 129

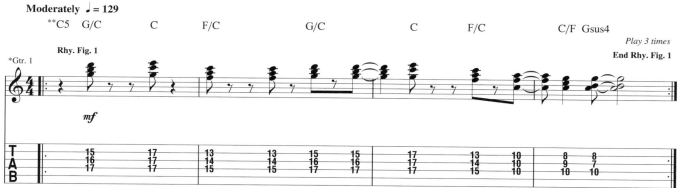

*Synth. arr. for gtr.

**Chord symbols reflect overall harmony.

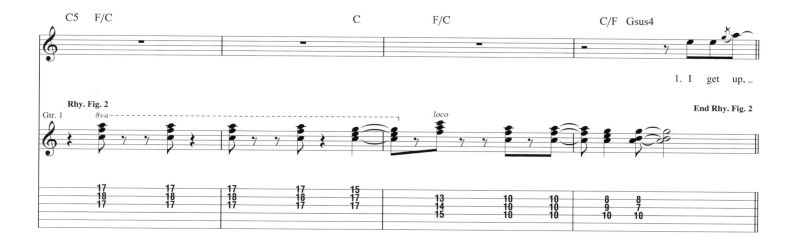

Gtr. 1: w/ Rhy. Fig. 1 (2 times)

C5 G/C   C   F/C   G/C   C   F/C   C/F Gsus4

___ Hey you!" _ "Who said that?" _ ba - by, just __ how you feel. __   You got to
                                   Ba - by how __ you been?   You say you don't

C5 G/C   C   F/C   G/C   C   F/C   C/F Gsus4

roll _____ with the punch - es and get to what's real. __   Ah, can't ya
know, _____ you won't __ know _____ un - til you be - gin. __   So can't ya

Pre-Chorus

Am
*(G#m)   F   C   Dm
                                                    (E)   (B)   (C#m)

see me stand - in' here, I got my back a - gainst the rec - ord ma - chine. _____

Gtr. 2 (dist.)

mf   *dim.*   P.M.   P.M. - - - - - - - - - -
rake - ┤

*Symbols in parentheses represent chord names respective to
altered tuned guitars. Symbols above reflect actual sounding chords.

                                                    F   C   Dm
                                                    (E)   (B)   (C#m)

I ain't the worst that you've seen. _____   Ah, can't ya see what I mean? _

P.M. - - - - - - - - - -┤   P.M. - - - - - - - - - ┤   P.M. - - -

126

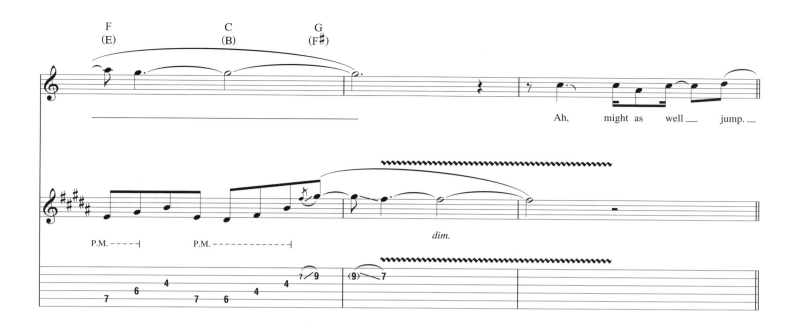

Ah, might as well __ jump. __

Chorus

Gtr. 1: w/ Rhy. Fig. 1
Gtr. 2 tacet

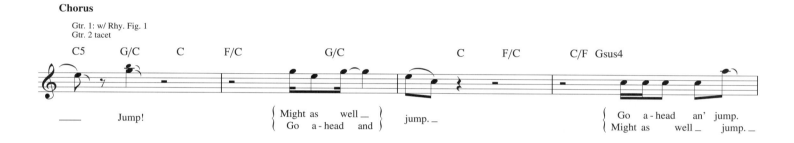

__ Jump!   { Might as well __ } jump. __   { Go a-head an' jump.
                { Go a-head and }   { Might as well __ jump. __

2nd time, Gtr. 1: w/ Rhy. Fig. 1

1.

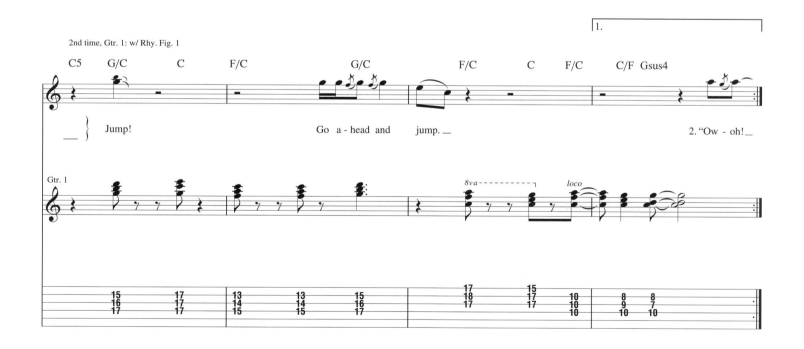

__ } Jump!   Go a-head and jump. __   2. "Ow - oh! __

Gtr. 1

Gtr. 1: w/ Riff A

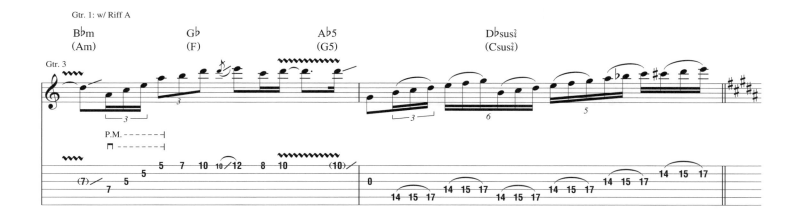

Synth. Solo

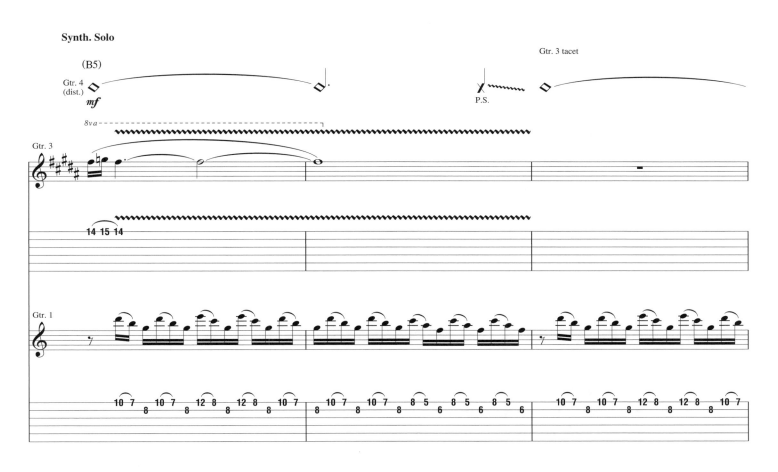

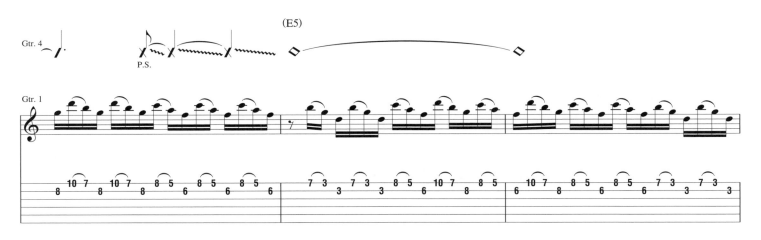

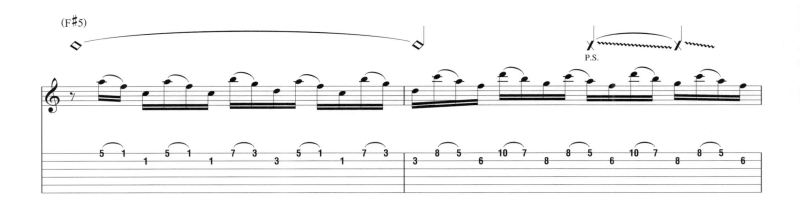

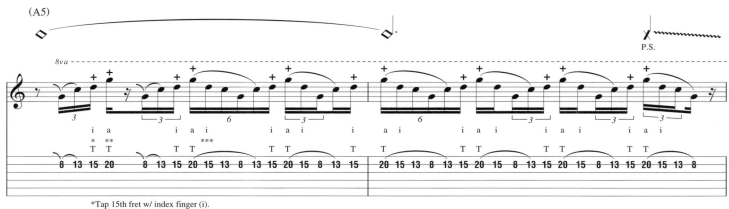

*Tap 15th fret w/ index finger (i).
**Tap 20th fret with ring finger (a).
***Pull off ring finger to index finger.

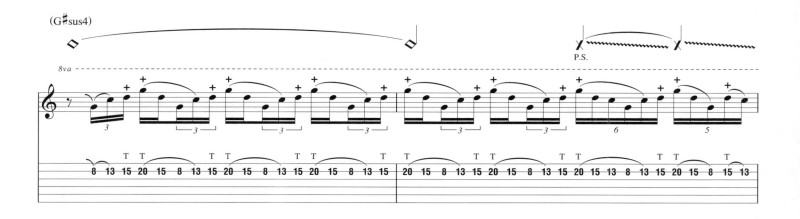

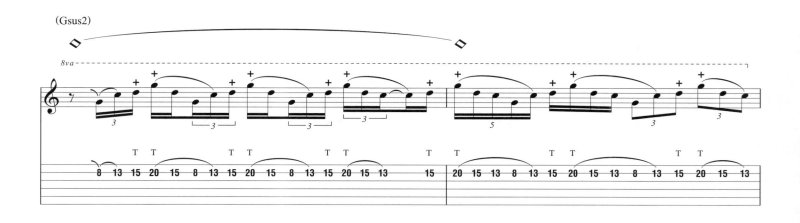

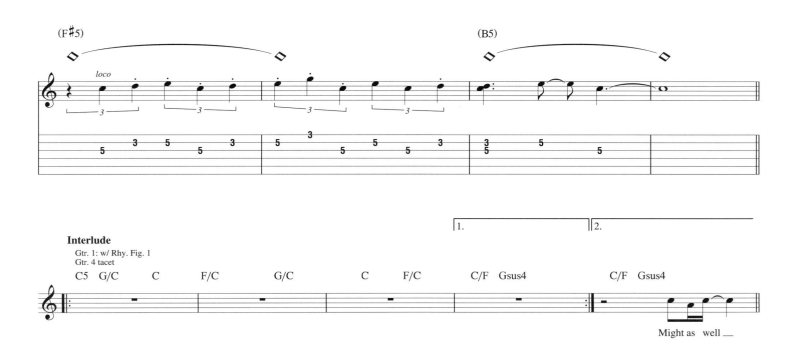

Interlude

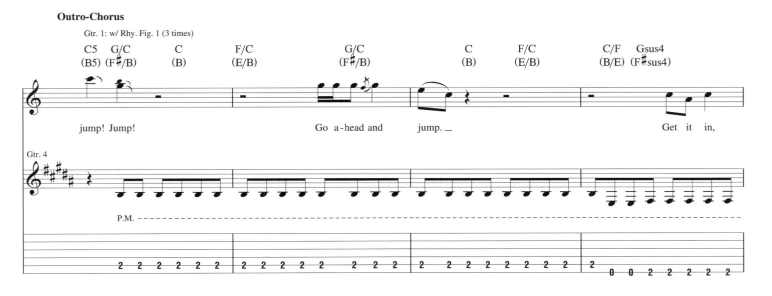

Outro-Chorus

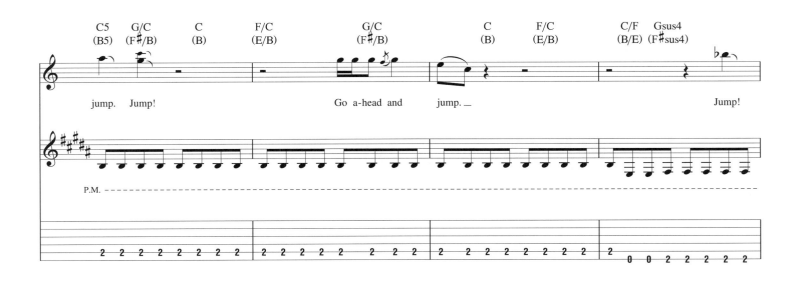

from *Van Halen*

Little Dreamer

Words and Music by David Lee Roth, Edward Van Halen, Alex Van Halen and Michael Anthony

Tune down 1/2 step:
(low to high) Eb-Ab-Db-Gb-Bb-Eb

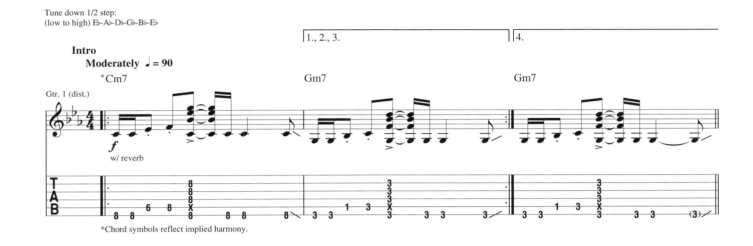

*Chord symbols reflect implied harmony.

2. And then they went and they vot - ed you least like - ly to suc - ceed.
3. Yeah, they talk a - bout you cold when you were head - ed for the skies,

I had, a, tell them, ba - by, you were armed with all you'd need, ah.
but you were young and bold and, ba - by, did - n't that change with a wink of your eye.

Seems no one's talk - in' 'bout those
Seems no one's talk - in' 'bout the

cra - zy days gone past.
cra - zy days gone past.

Weren't they a - mazed when you were real - ly last?

Chorus

Cm7   Gm7   Fm7

You are the lit-tle dream-er.

(Oo.

P.M.

slight P.H.

To Coda

G7   Cm7   Gm7

You were __   the lit-tle __

Oo.)

w/ bar   w/ bar   w/ bar P.M.   w/ bar

Fm7   G

dream - er.   Yeah,   e,   yeah.

slight P.H.   w/ bar grad. dive

Fill 3
Gtr. 1   (to Coda)

Harm. slight P.H.

Pitch: A

136

Guitar Solo

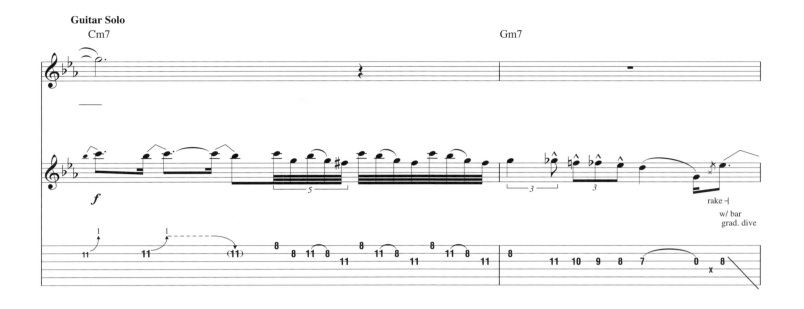

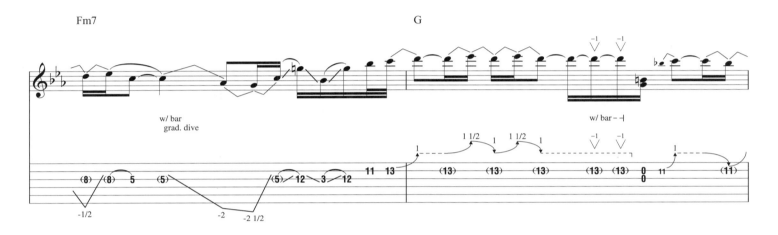

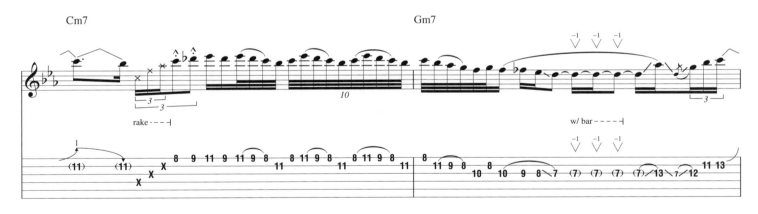

D.S. al Coda

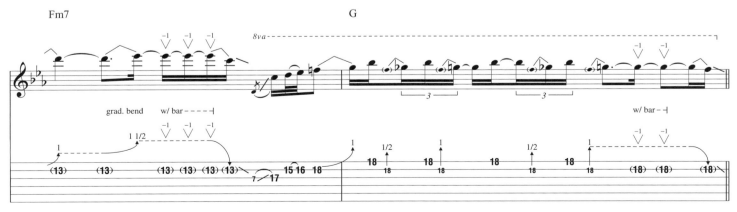

from *Fair Warning*

Mean Street

Words and Music by David Lee Roth, Edward Van Halen, Alex Van Halen and Michael Anthony

Tune down 1/2 step:
(low to high) E♭-A♭-D♭-G♭-B♭-E♭

Intro

Moderately fast ♩ = 132

N.C.

Play 3 times

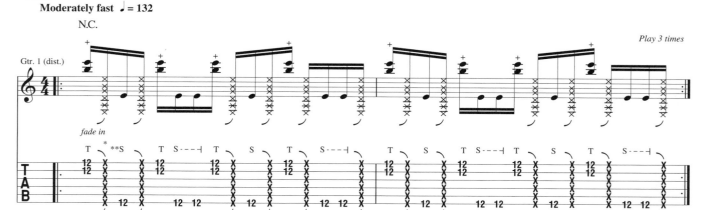

fade in

*Hammer-on mute strings w/ fingers of left hand.
**Slap 6th string w/ right hand thumb.

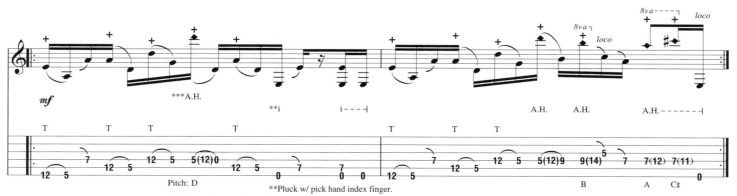

Pitch: D

**Pluck w/ pick hand index finger.

***Artificial harmonic produced by tapping
the parenthetical fret numbers while fretting the 5th fret.

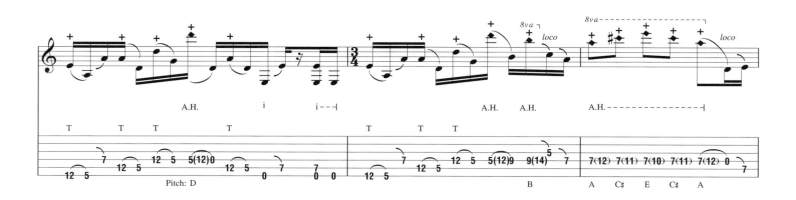

Pitch: D

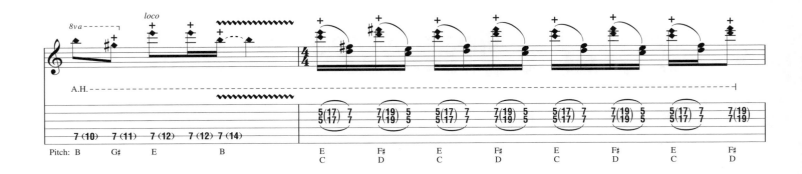

Free time

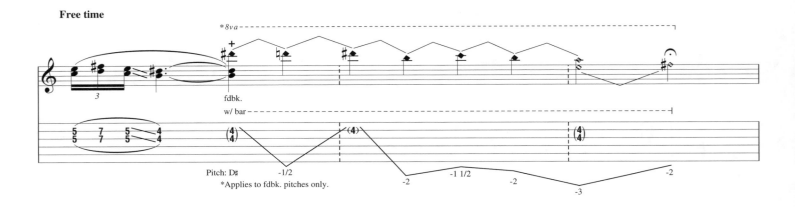

Slower ♩ = 100

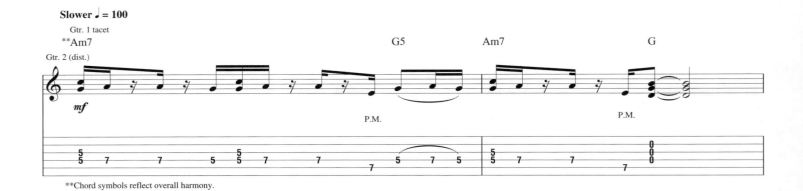

**Chord symbols reflect overall harmony.

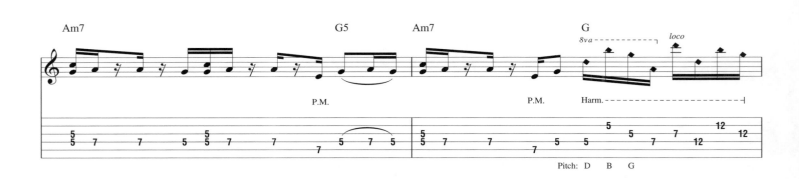

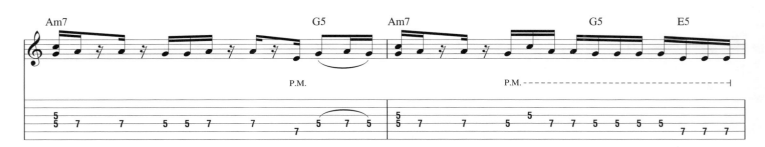

Lyrics:
1. At night I walk this ___ stink-in' street, past the cra-zies on ___ my block, ___ and I see the same ___ old fac-es and I hear ___ that same old talk. And I'm search-ing for ___ the lat-est thing, a break in ___ this rou-tine. ___ I'm talk-in' some ___ new kicks, ones ___ like a

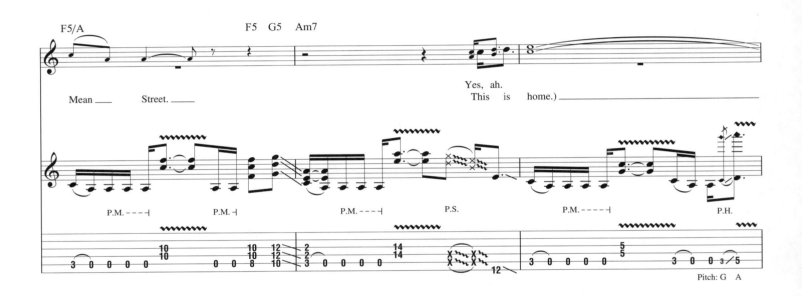

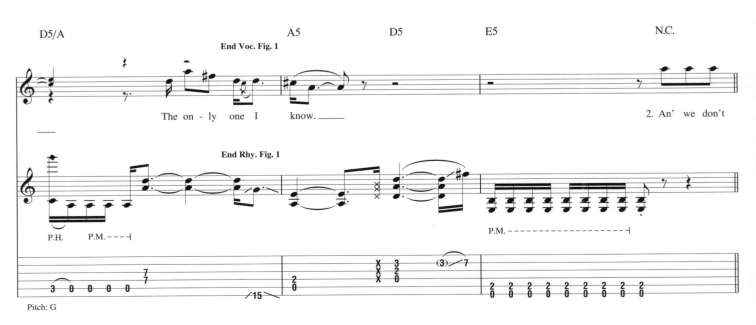

Verse

Gtr. 2: w/ Riff A (4 times)

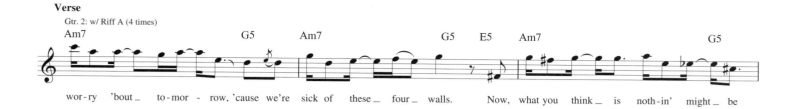

wor-ry 'bout _ to-mor - row, 'cause we're sick of these _ four _ walls. Now, what you think _ is noth-in' might be

some-thin' af - ter all. _ Now, you know _ this ain't _ no through _ street, _ the end _ is dead _ a - head. _ The

Chorus

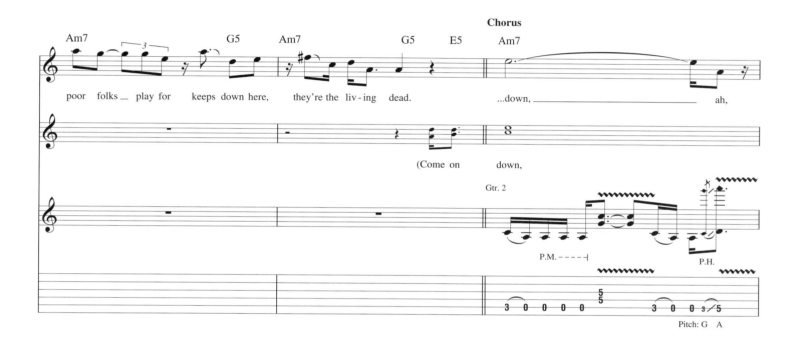

poor folks _ play for keeps down here, they're the liv-ing dead.   ...down, _____ ah,

(Come on   down,

Gtr. 2

Pitch: G   A

huh,   ow,   down __ to Mean _ Street.   They're danc - in'

this   is   Mean _ Street.   Danc - in'

Pitch: G   A

143

now,   look, _____   out ___ on Mean _ Street.

now   out   on Mean _ Street.)

P.M. - - - -｜   P.M. P.H.   P.M. - - - -｜   string
noise

Pitch: E F#

Interlude

A5

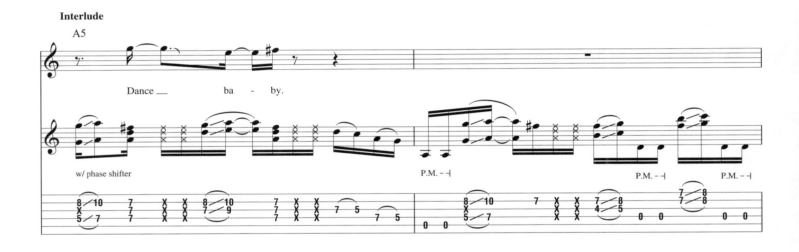

Dance ___   ba - by.

w/ phase shifter   P.M. -｜   P.M. -｜   P.M. -｜

P.M. -｜   P.M. -｜   P.M. -｜

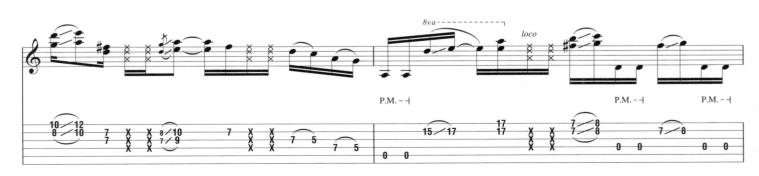

8va - - - - - - - - - - - - -｜   loco

P.M. -｜   P.M. -｜   P.M. -｜

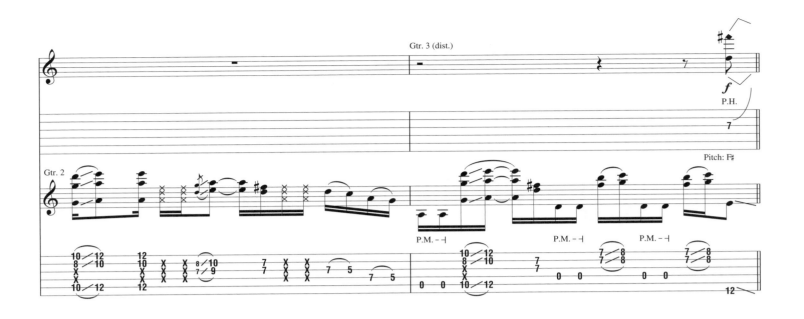

Guitar Solo

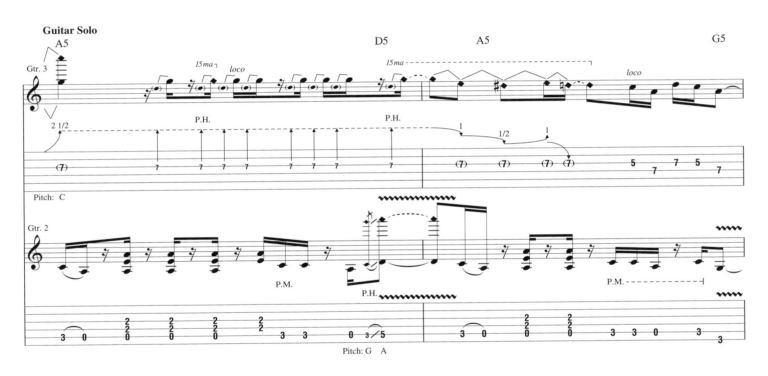

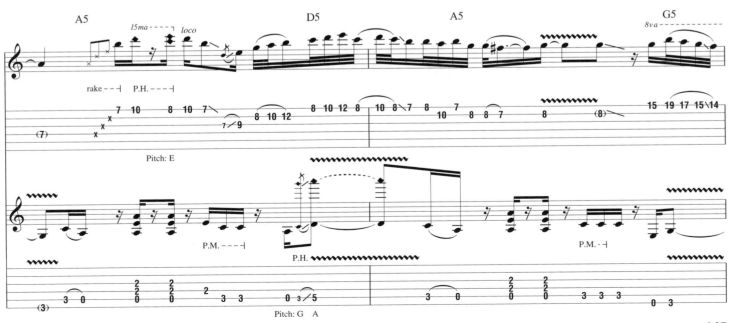

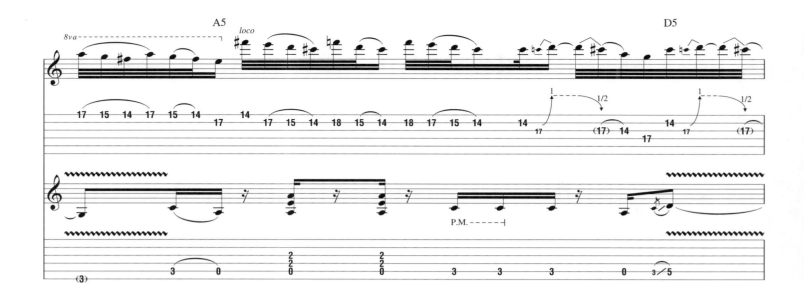

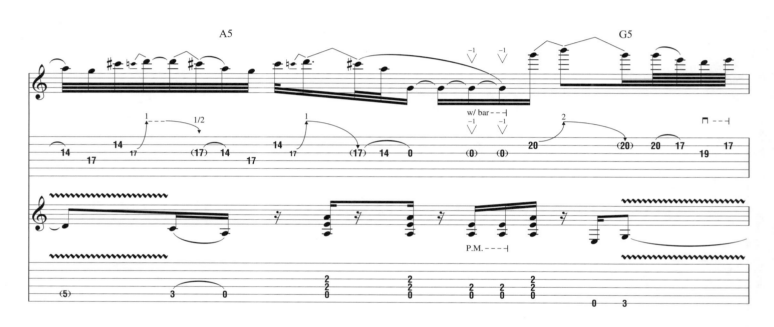

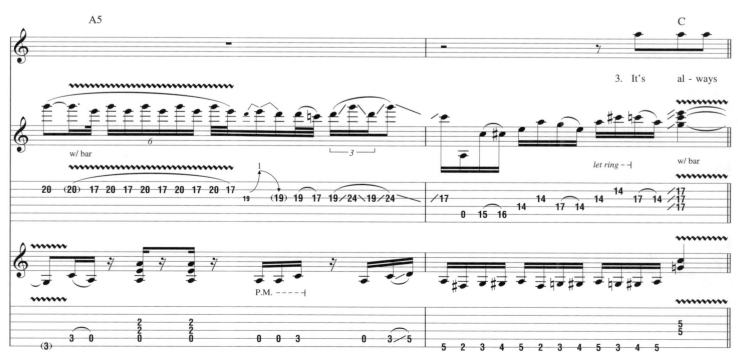

3. It's always

Verse

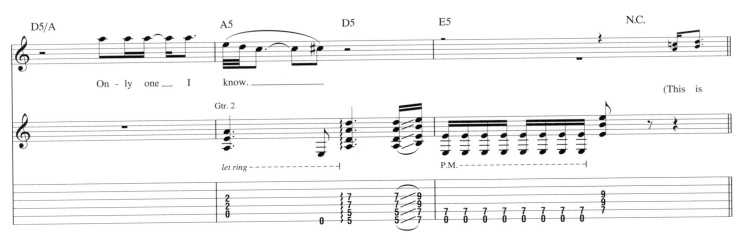

Bridge

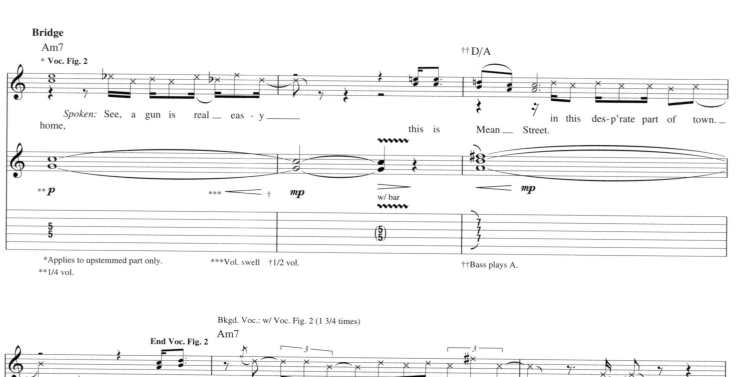

*Applies to upstemmed part only.   ***Vol. swell   †1/2 vol.   ††Bass plays A.
**1/4 vol.

†††3/4 vol.

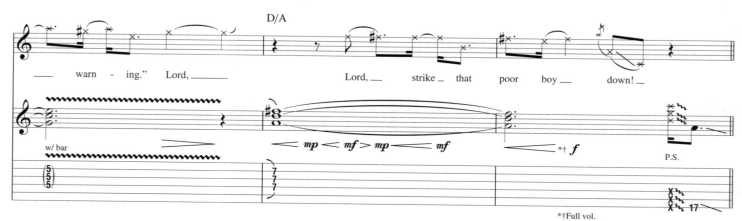

*†Full vol.

Interlude

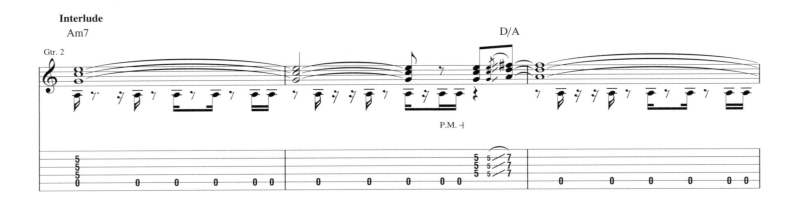

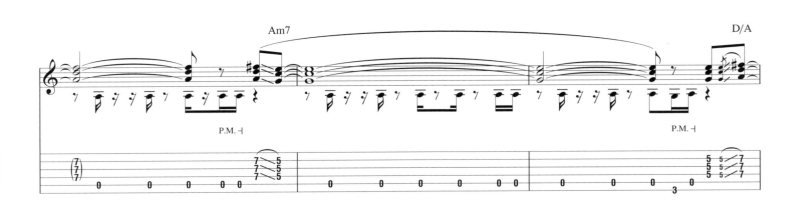

Outro-Guitar Solo

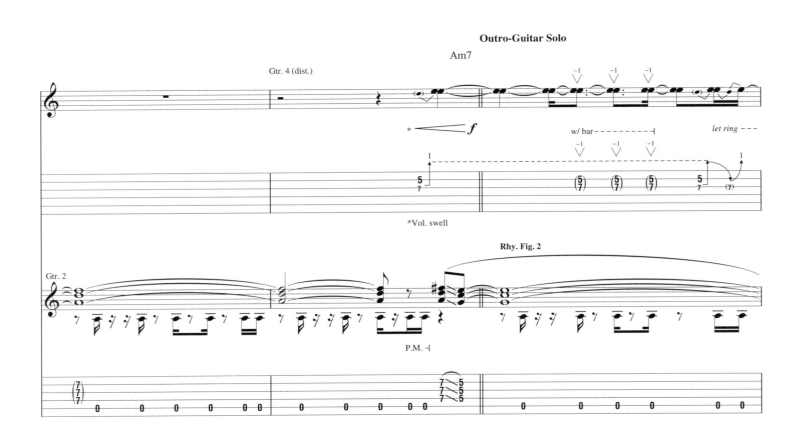

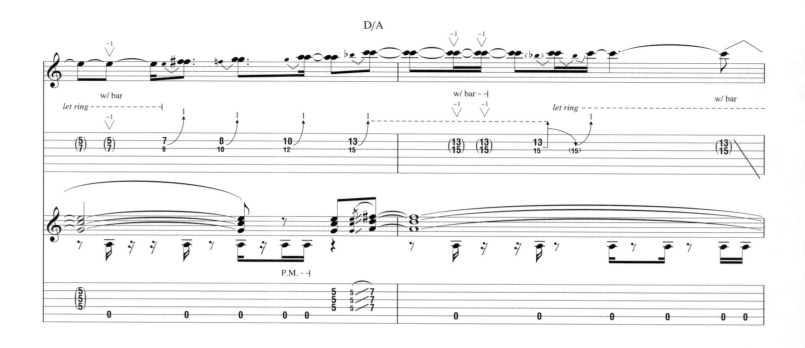

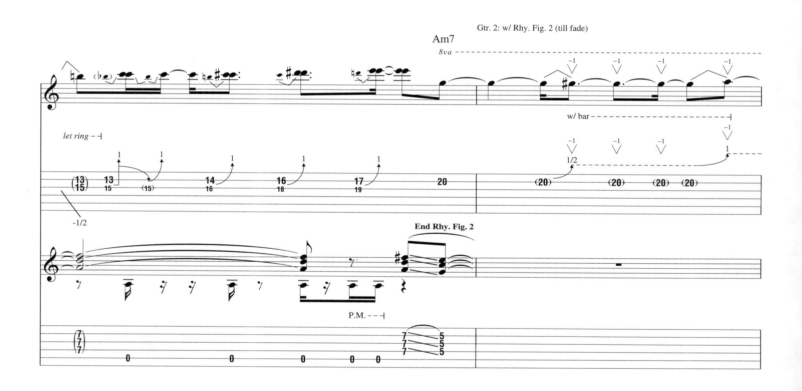

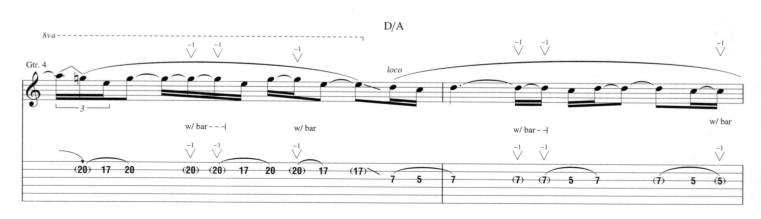

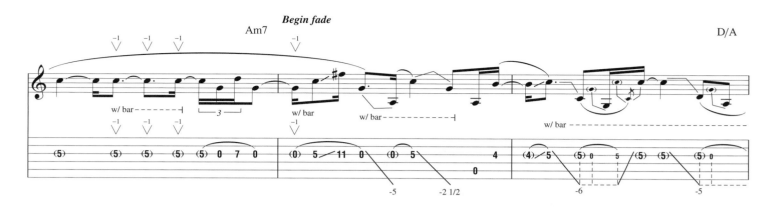

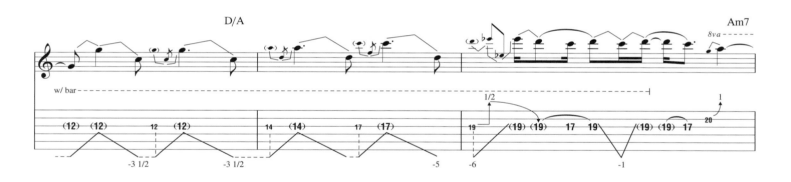

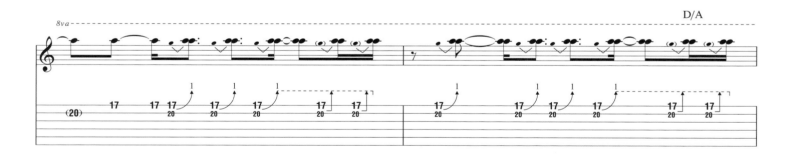

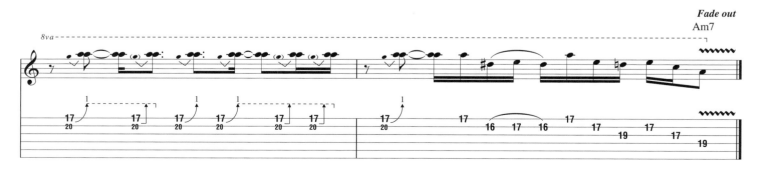

from *1984*

Panama

Words and Music by David Lee Roth, Edward Van Halen, Alex Van Halen and Michael Anthony

Tune down 1/2 step:
(low to high) E♭-A♭-D♭-G♭-B♭-E♭

Intro
Moderate Rock ♩ = 144

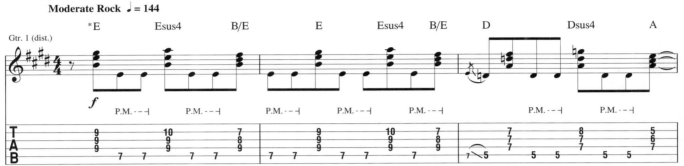

*Chord symbols reflect basic harmony.

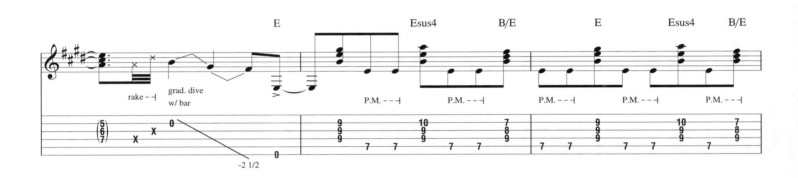

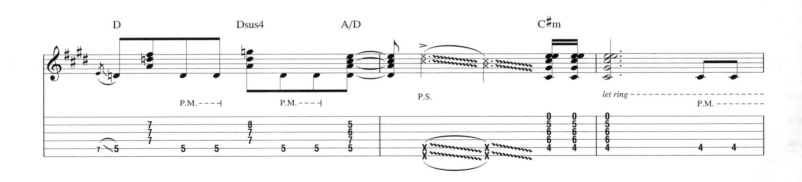

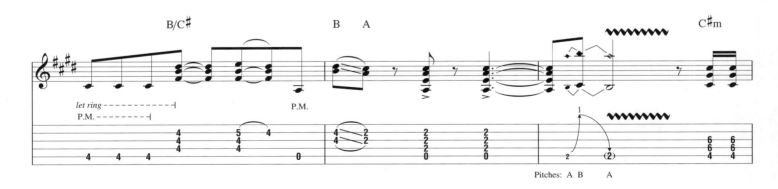

Pitches: A B   A

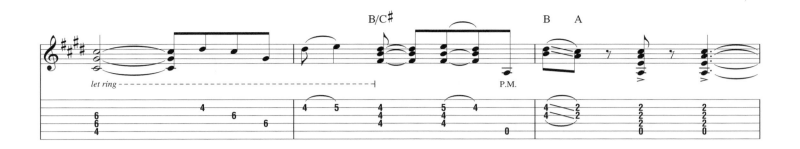

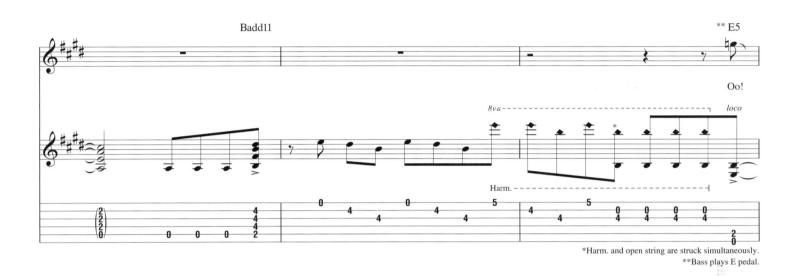

*Harm. and open string are struck simultaneously.
**Bass plays E pedal.

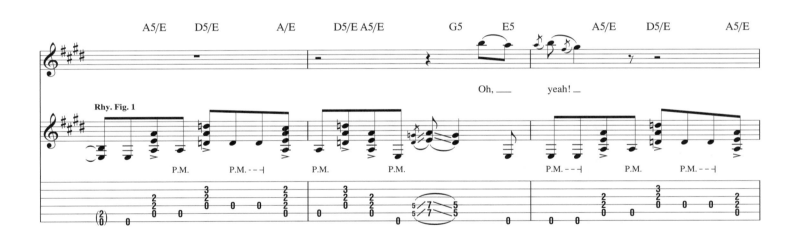

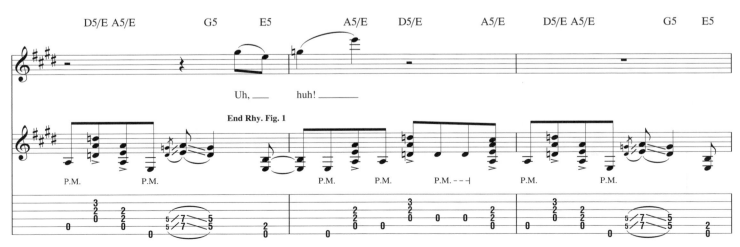

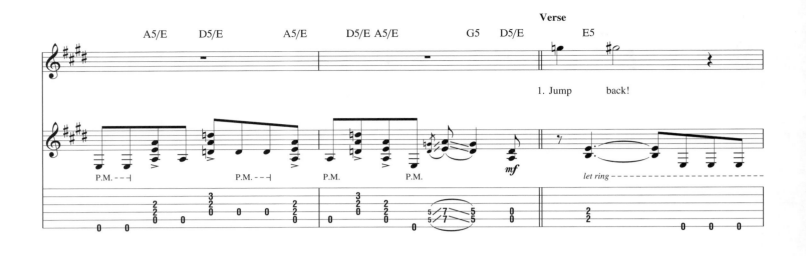

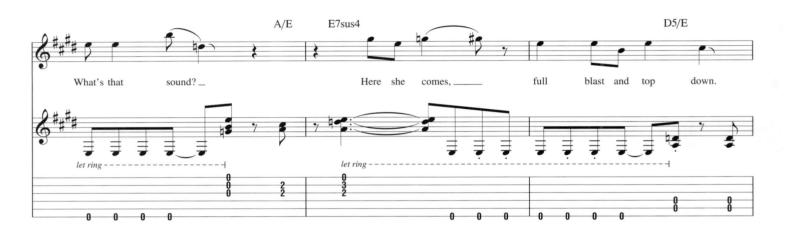

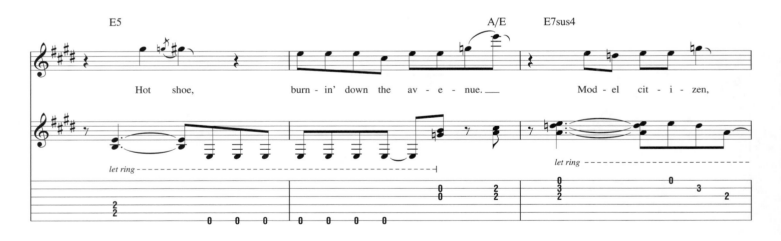

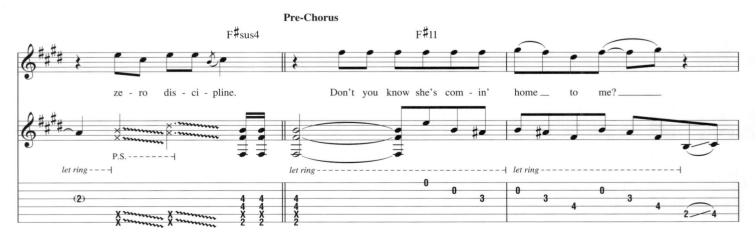

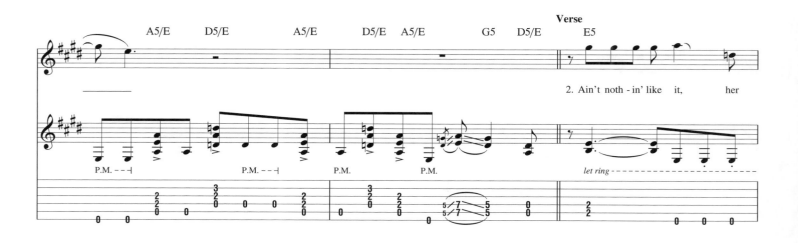

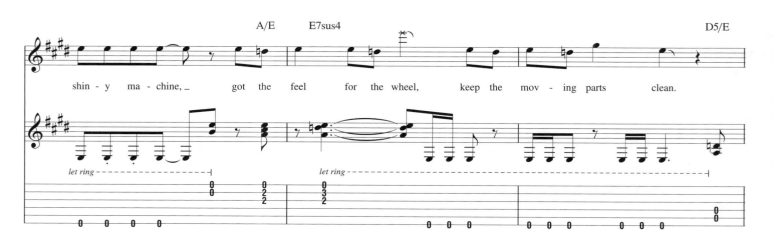

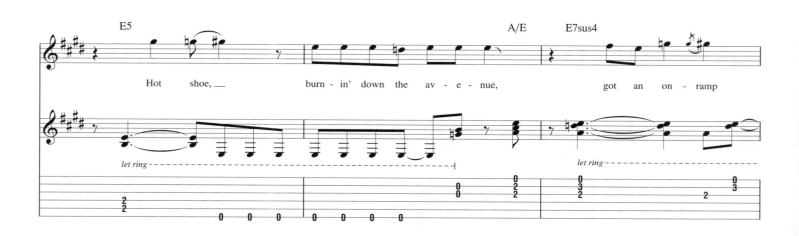

Pre-Chorus

You'll lose her in the ___ turn. ___ I'll get her! _____

Wuh ___ oh! Pan - a - ma,

Chorus
Gtr. 1: w/ Rhy. Fig. 1

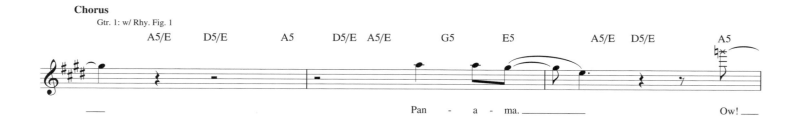

___ Pan - a - ma. _____ Ow! ___

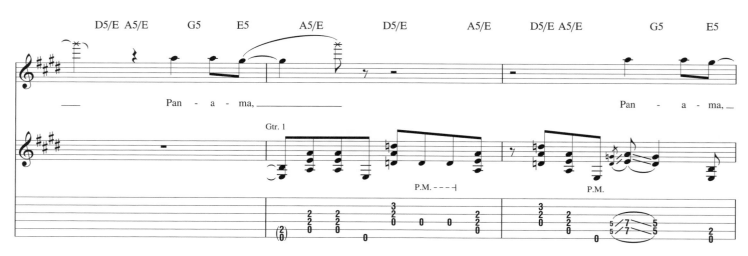

___ Pan - a - ma, _____ Pan - a - ma, ___

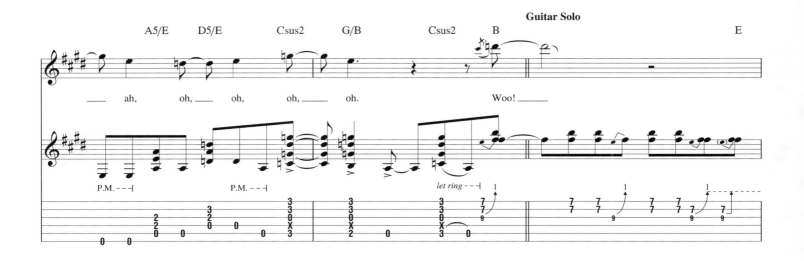

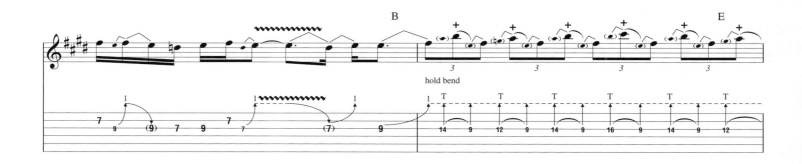

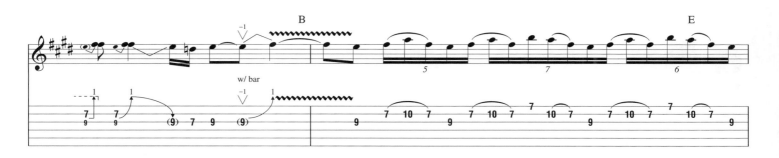

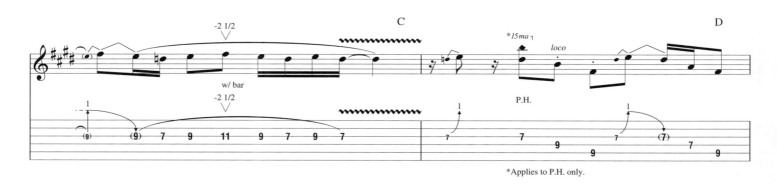

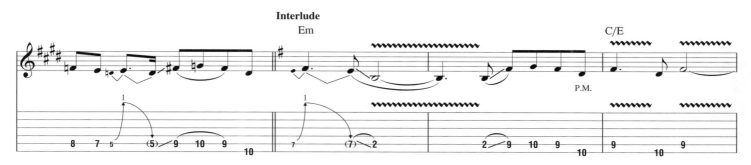

158

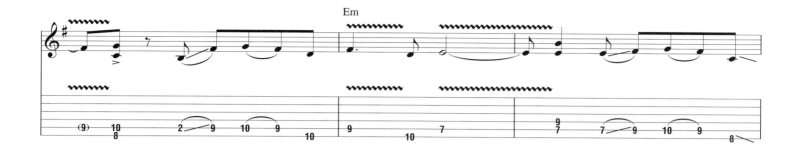

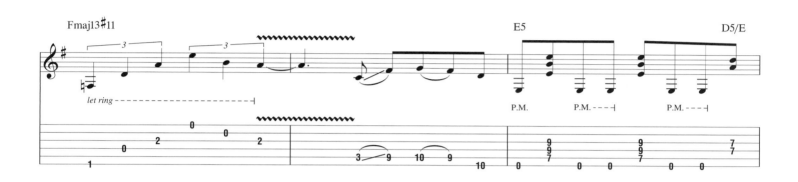

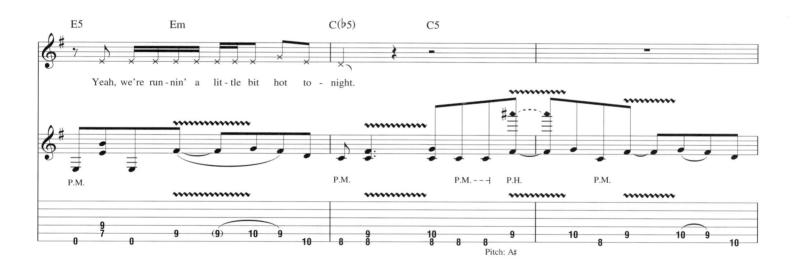

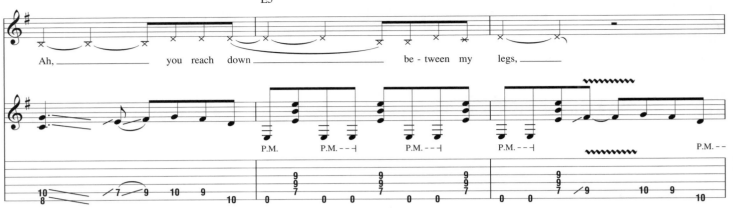

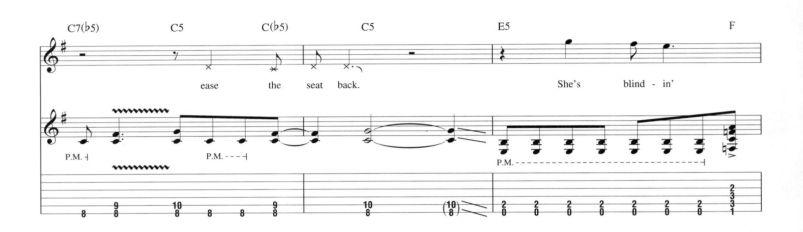

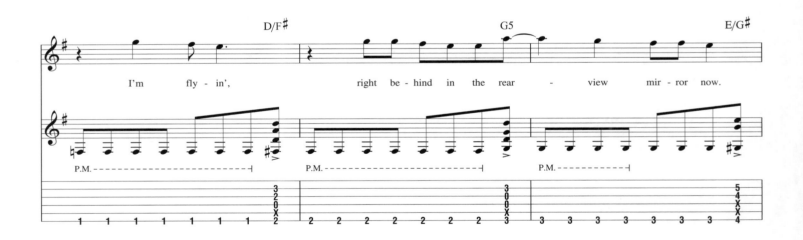

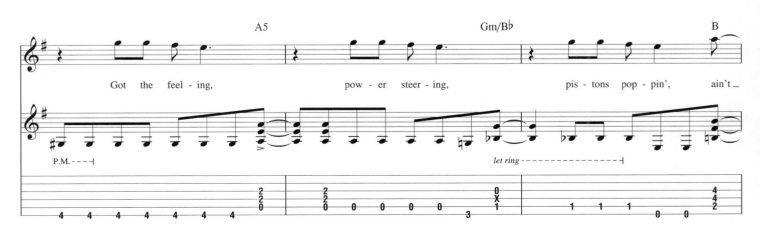

160

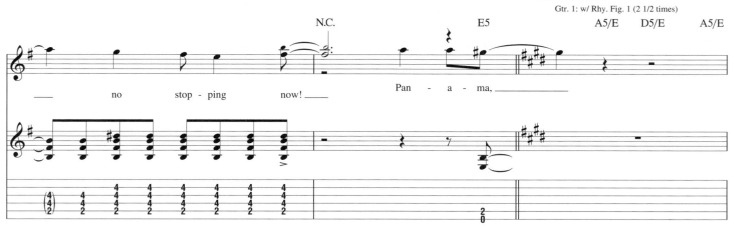

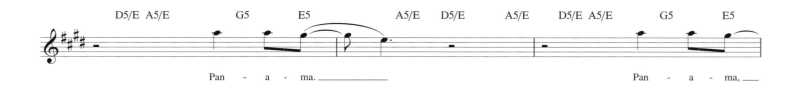

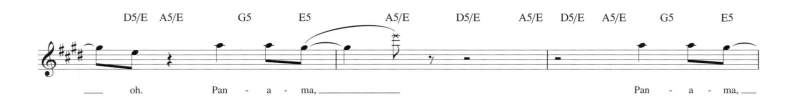

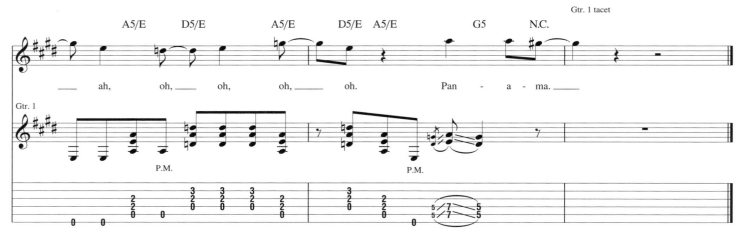

from *Van Halen*

Runnin' with the Devil

Words and Music by David Lee Roth, Edward Van Halen, Alex Van Halen and Michael Anthony

Tune down 1/2 step:
(low to high) E♭-A♭-D♭-G♭-B♭-E♭

Intro
Moderately ♩ = 104

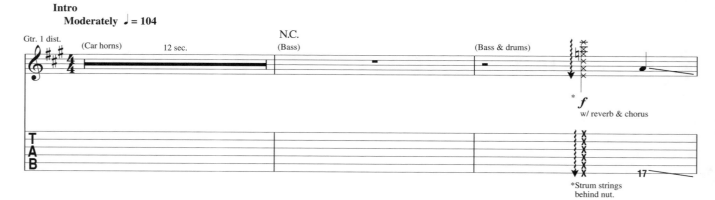

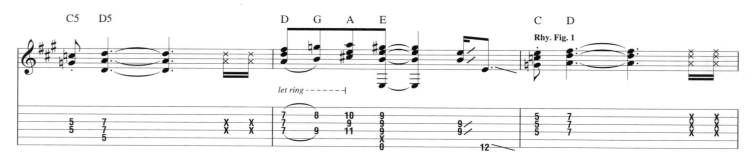

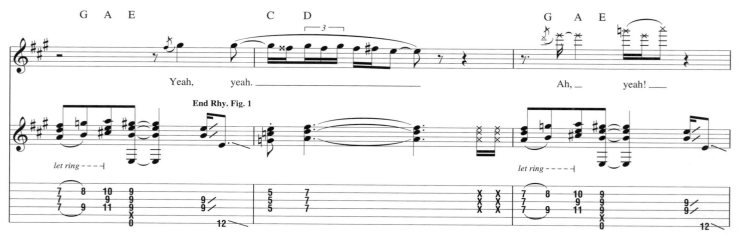

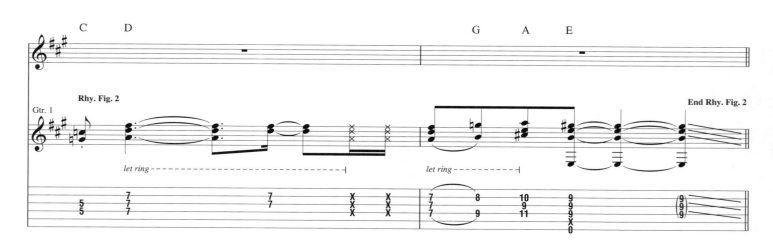

Chorus

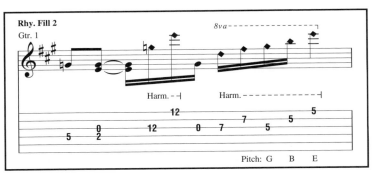

from *Van Halen II*

Somebody Get Me a Doctor

Words and Music by David Lee Roth, Edward Van Halen, Alex Van Halen and Michael Anthony

Tune down 1/2 step:
(low to high) E♭-A♭-D♭-G♭-B♭-E♭

Intro
Moderately ♩ = 130

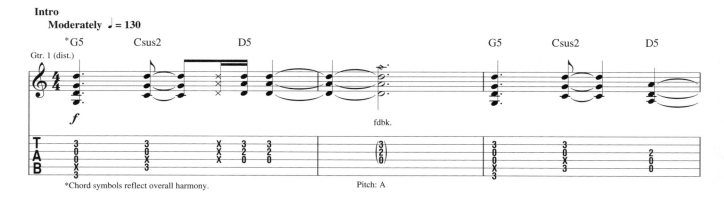

*Chord symbols reflect overall harmony.

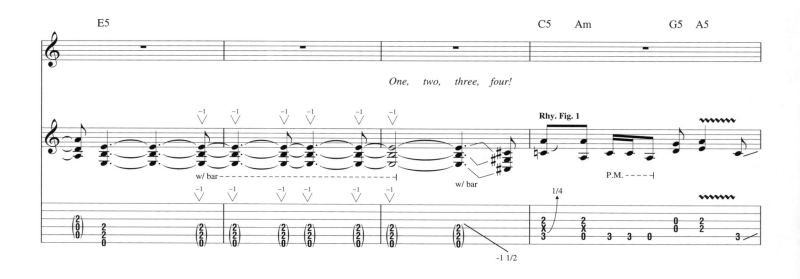

One, two, three, four!

Oo,

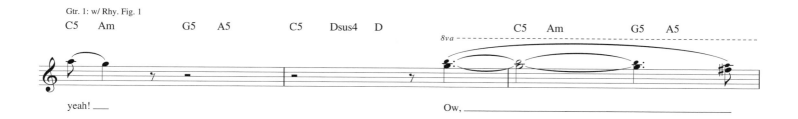

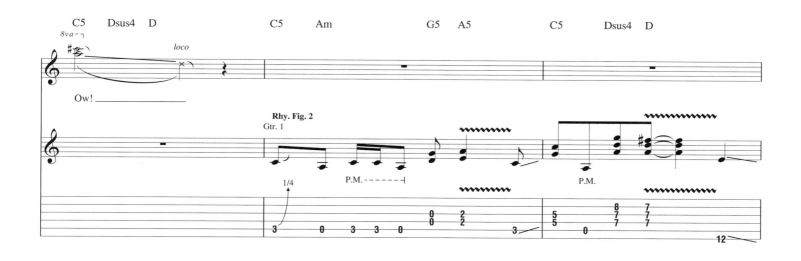

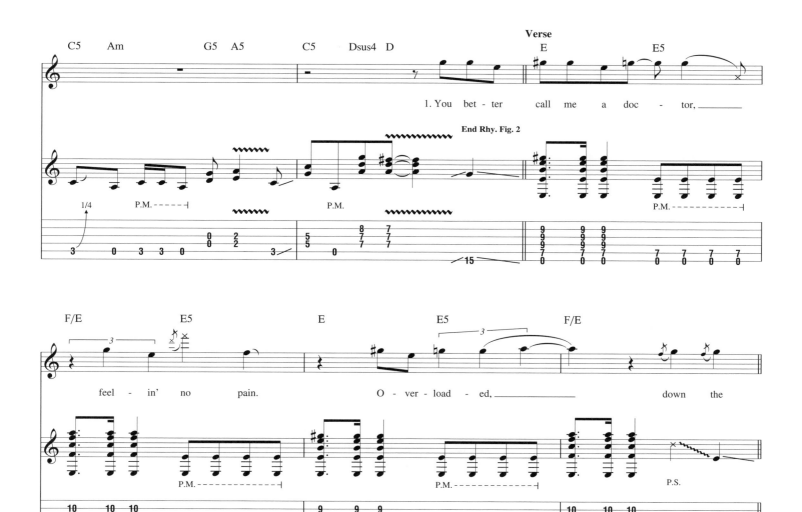

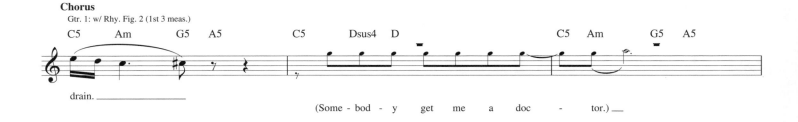

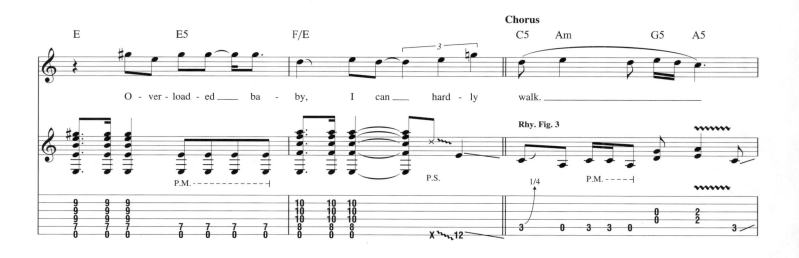

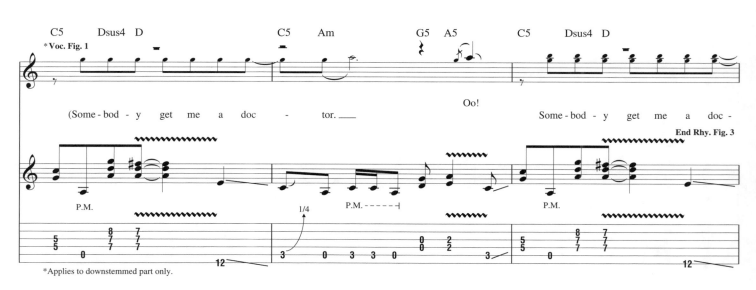

*Applies to downstemmed part only.

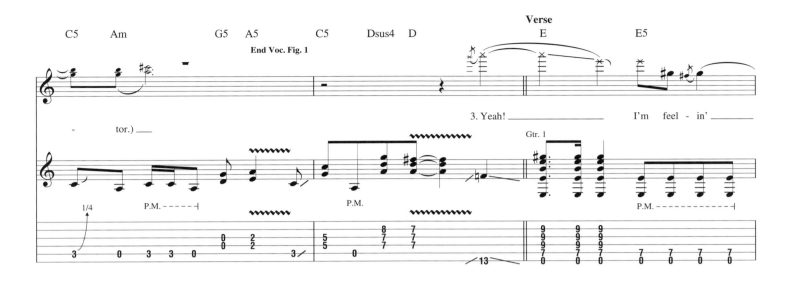

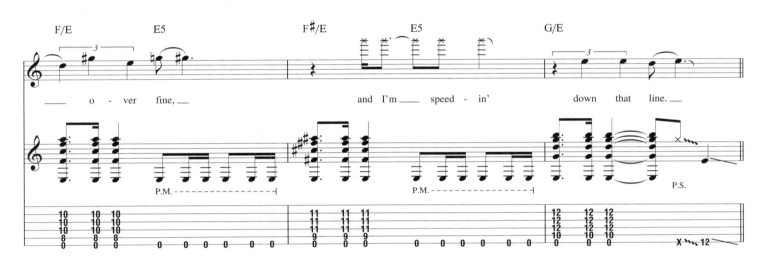

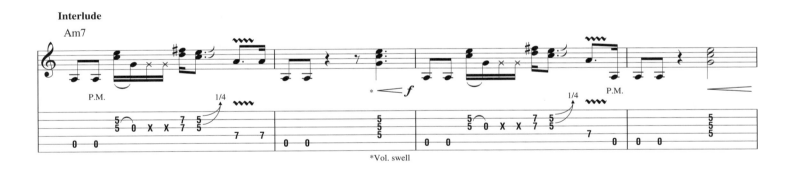

Guitar Solo

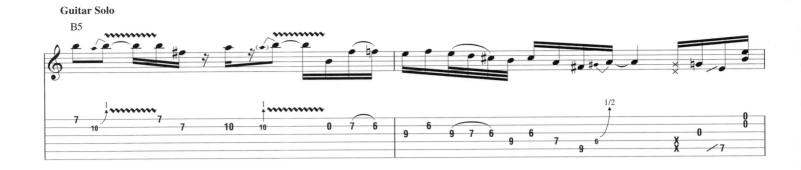

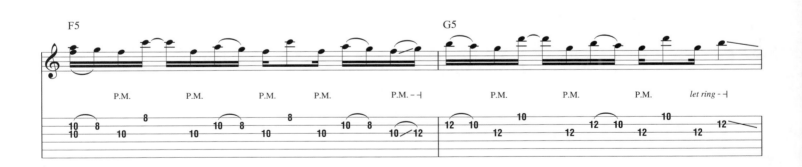

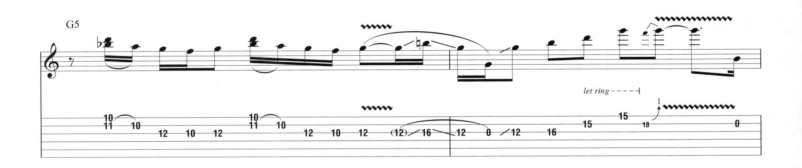

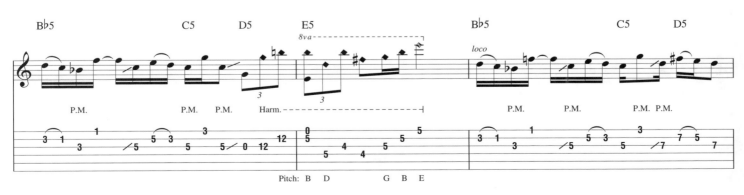

Free time

Bkgd. Voc.: w/ voc. ad lib (next 3 meas.)

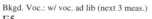

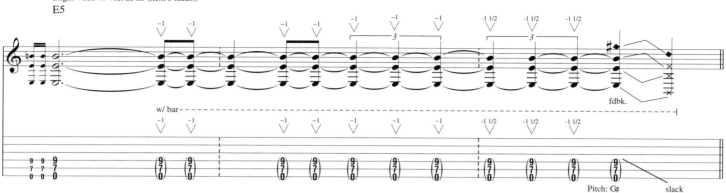

w/ bar

Pitch: G#   slack

Interlude

A tempo

Gtr. 1: w/ Rhy. Fig. 1 (1 1/2 times)

| C5 | Am | G5 | A5 | | C5 | Dsus4 | D | | C5 | Am | G5 | A5 |

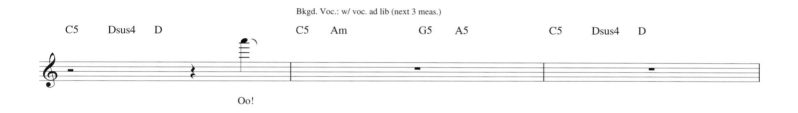

Bkgd. Voc.: w/ voc. ad lib (next 3 meas.)

| C5 | Dsus4 | D | | C5 | Am | G5 | A5 | | C5 | Dsus4 | D |

Oo!

C5   Am N.C.

Gtr. 1

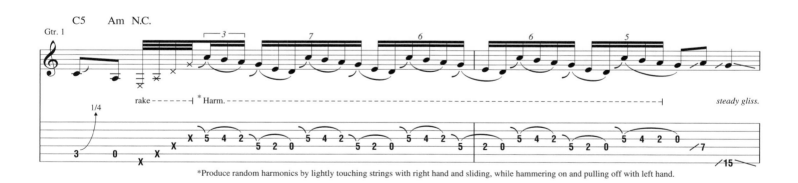

rake ——— *Harm. ———————————————————————   steady gliss.

1/4

*Produce random harmonics by lightly touching strings with right hand and sliding, while hammering on and pulling off with left hand.

Gtr. 1: w/ Rhy. Fig. 2

| C5 | Am | G5 | A5 | | C5 | Dsus4 | D | | C5 | Am | G5 | A5 | | C5 | Dsus4 | D |

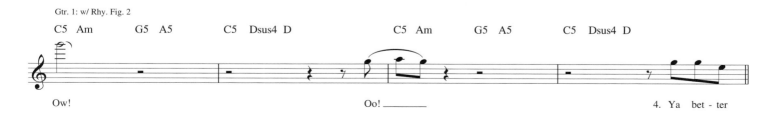

Ow!   Oo! _____   4. Ya bet - ter

Verse

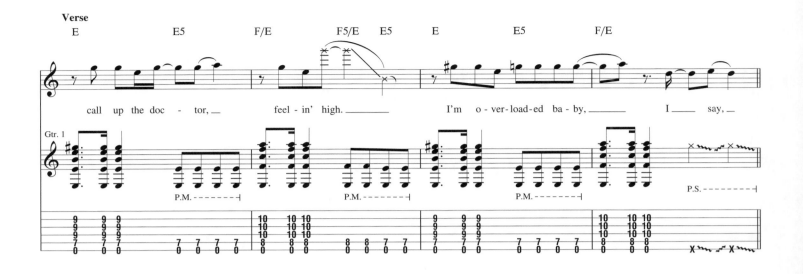

call up the doc - tor, _____ feel - in' high. _____ I'm o - ver - load - ed ba - by, _____ I __ say, __

Chorus

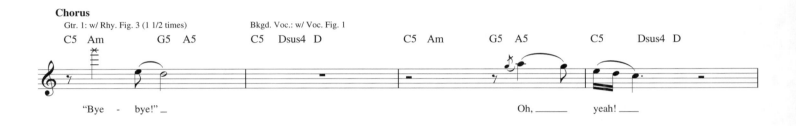

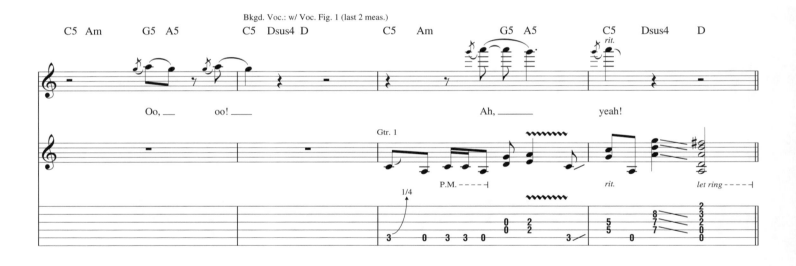

"Bye - bye!" __   Oh, _____ yeah! __

Oo, __ oo! __   Ah, _____ yeah!

Outro
Free time

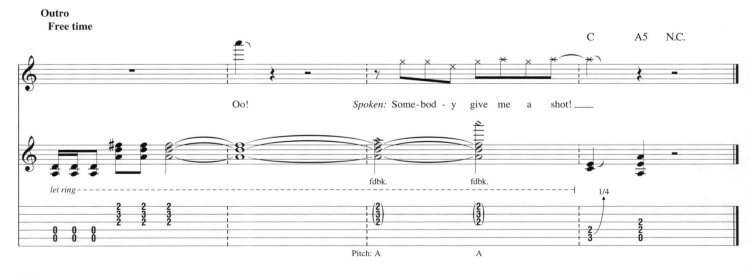

Oo!   *Spoken:* Some - bod - y give me a shot! __

from *Van Halen II*

Spanish Fly

Words and Music by David Lee Roth, Edward Van Halen, Alex Van Halen and Michael Anthony

*Chord symbols reflect implied harmony.
**Artificial harmonics produced by tapping strings 12 frets above open strings or fretted notes.

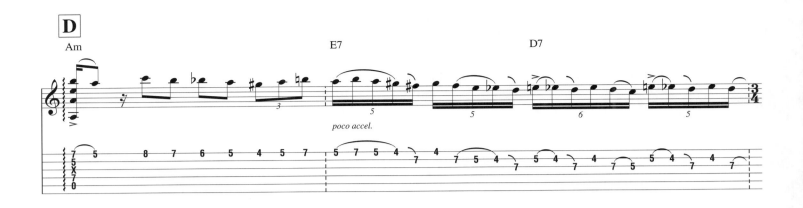

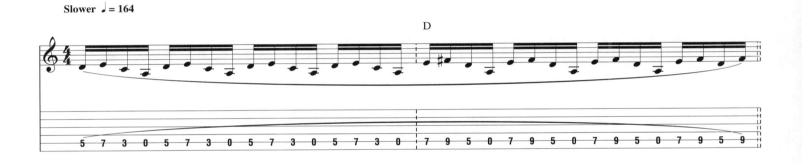

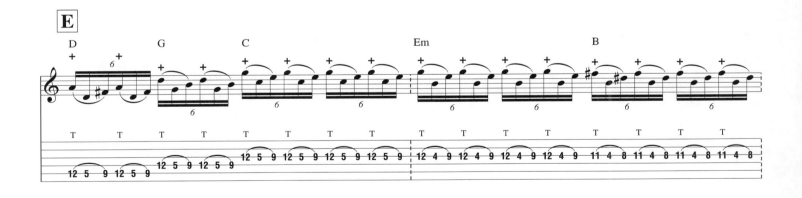

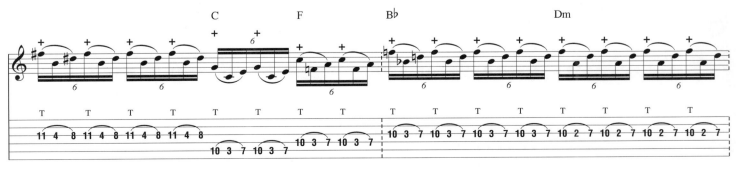

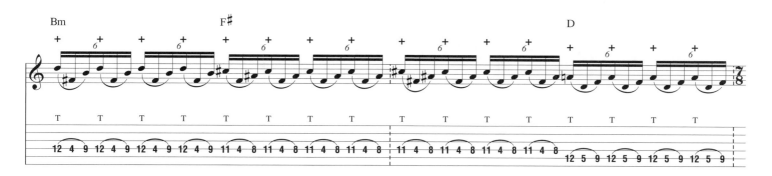

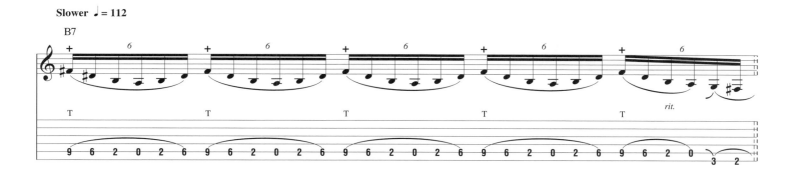

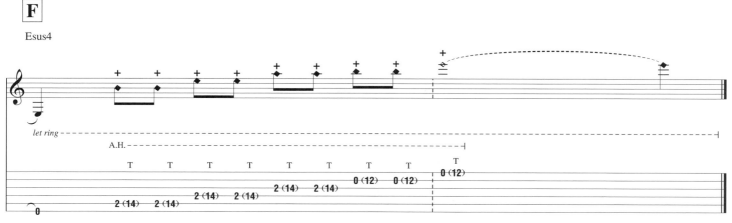

from *1984*
Top Jimmy

Words and Music by David Lee Roth, Edward Van Halen, Alex Van Halen and Michael Anthony

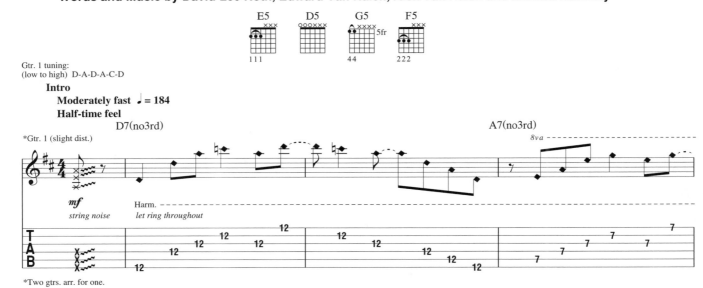

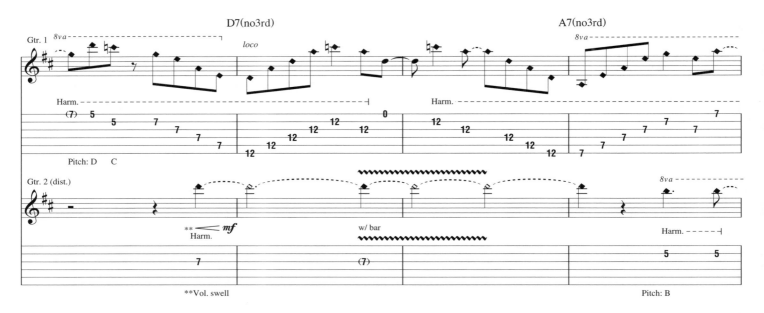

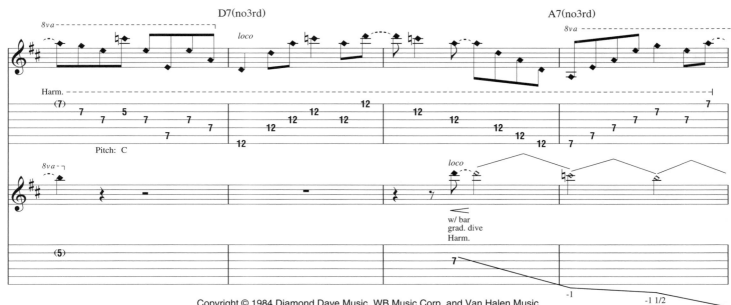

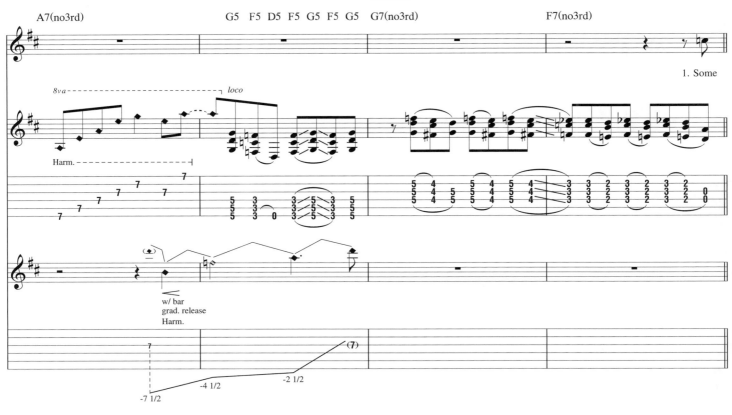

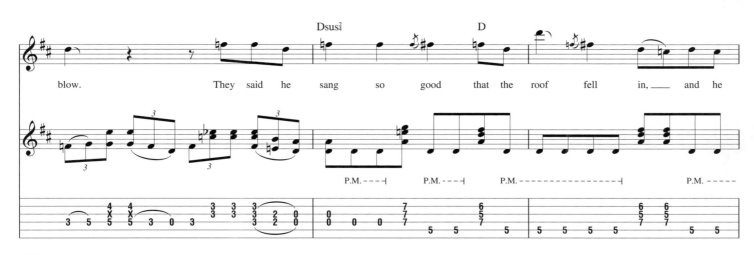

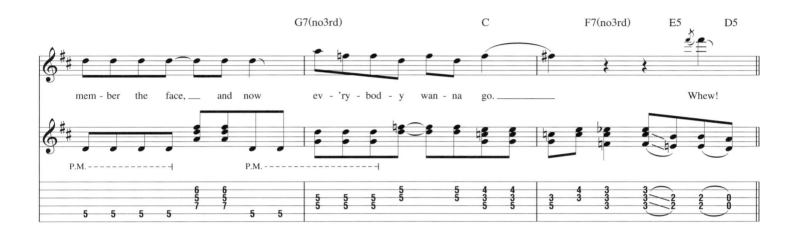

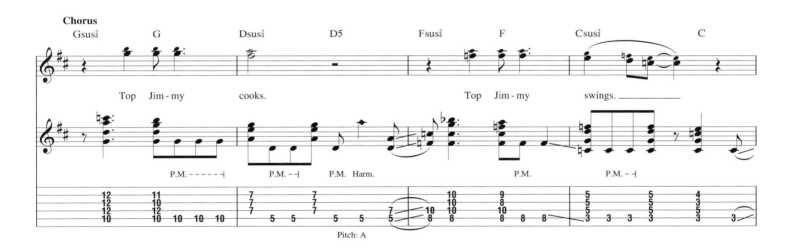

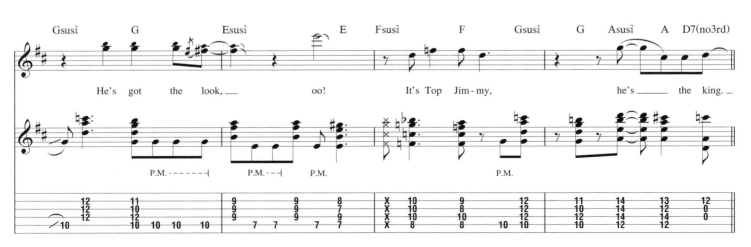

Interlude
Half-time feel

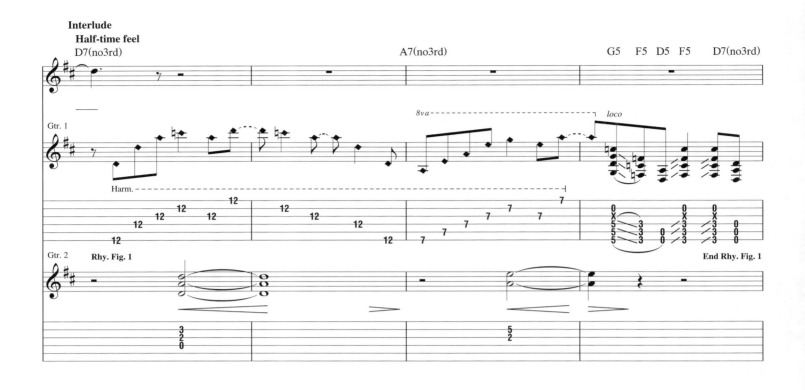

Gtr. 2: w/ Rhy. Fig. 1 (2 times)

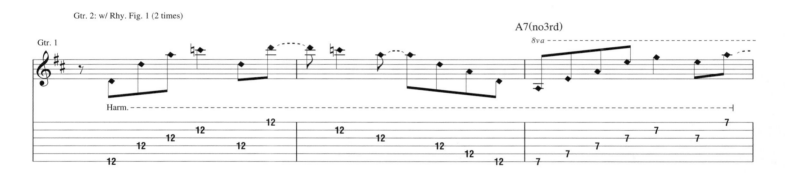

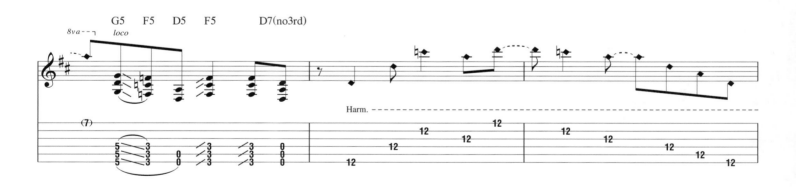

End half-time feel

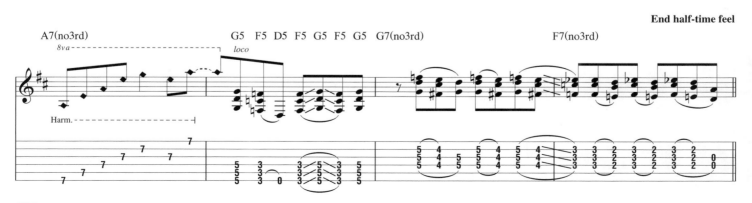

Verse

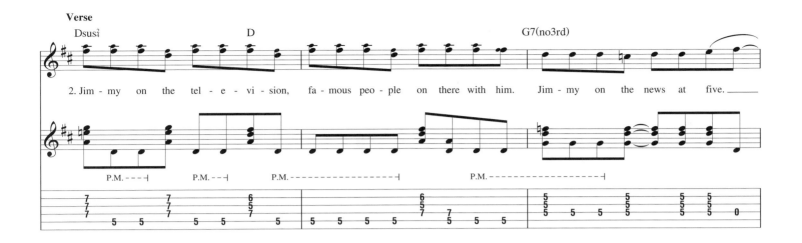

2. Jim - my on the tel - e - vi - sion, fa - mous peo - ple on there with him. Jim - my on the news at five._____

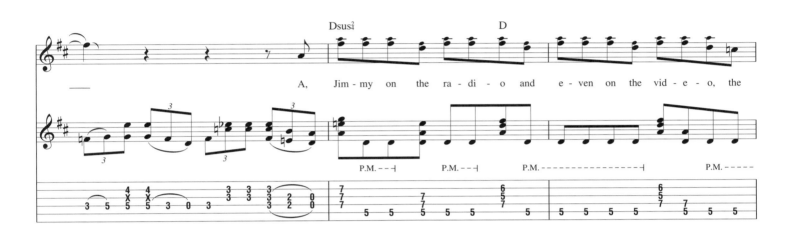

_____ A, Jim - my on the ra - di - o and e - ven on the vid - e - o, the

bad - dest cat ___ a - live. _____ A, driv - in' all the wom - en cra - zy,

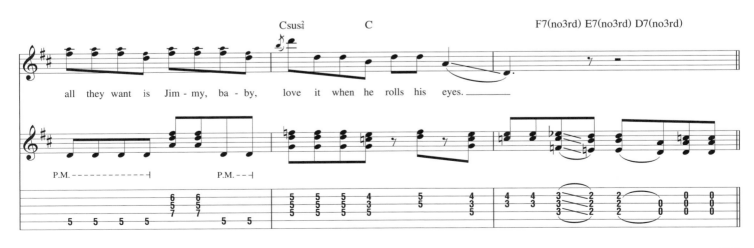

all they want is Jim - my, ba - by, love it when he rolls his eyes. _____

Chorus

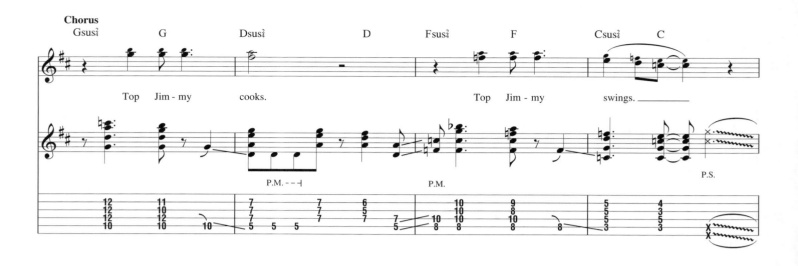

Top Jim - my cooks. Top Jim - my swings. _____

He's got the look, _____ Top Jim - my, whoo, shake it ba - by. _____

Guitar Solo

Half-time feel

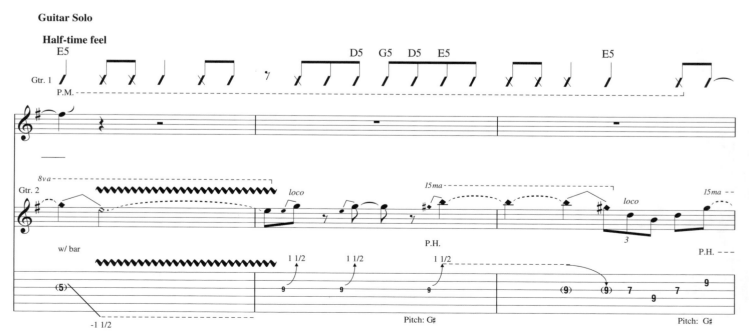

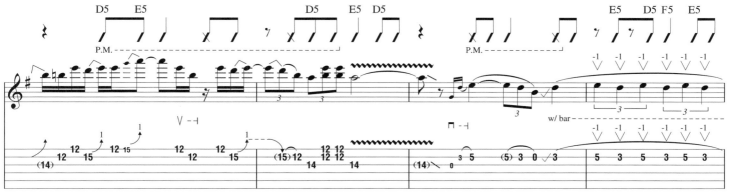

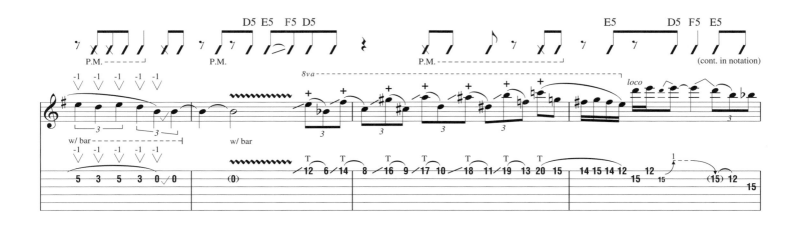

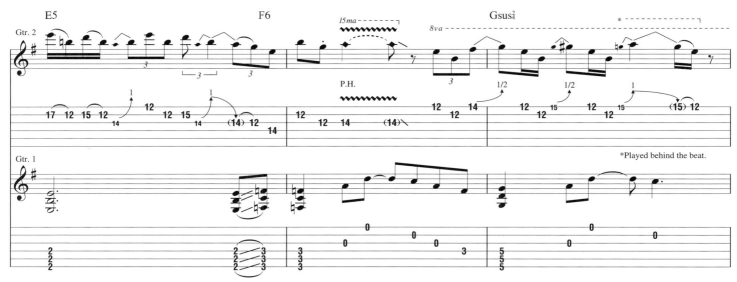

*Played behind the beat.

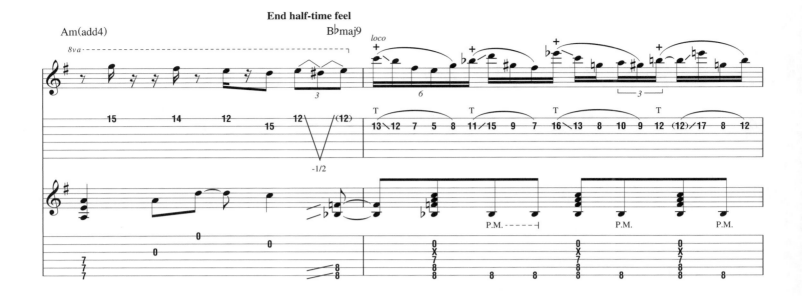

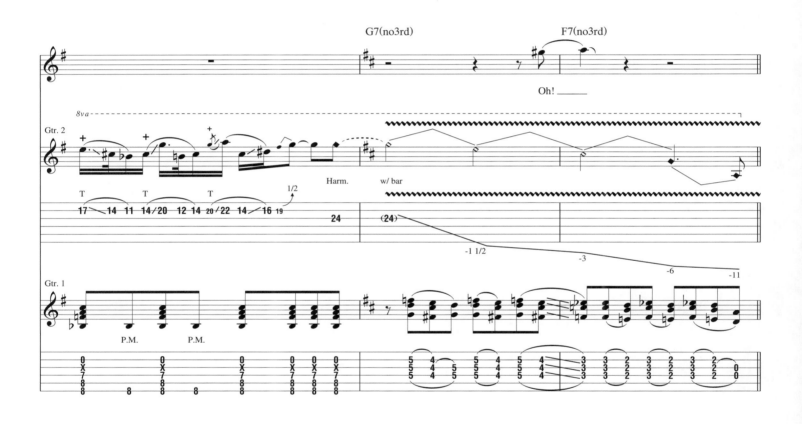

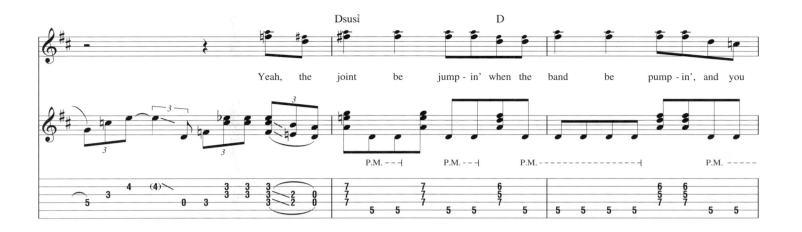

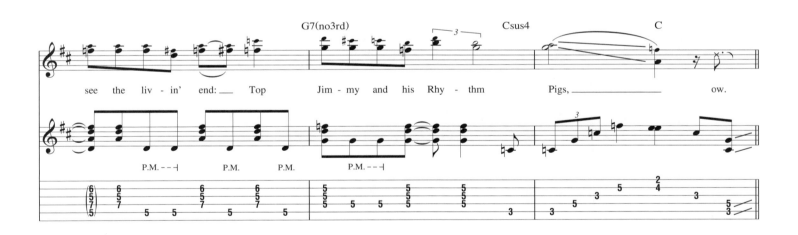

Chorus

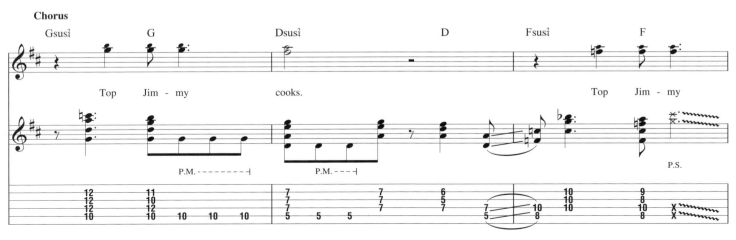

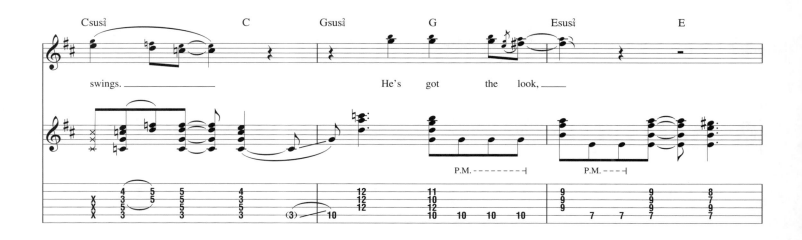

swings. _____ He's got the look, _____

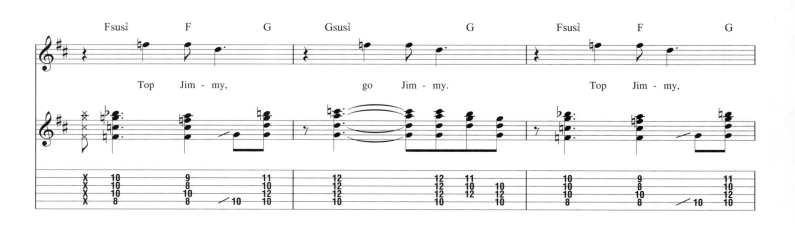

Top Jim - my,   go Jim - my.   Top Jim - my,

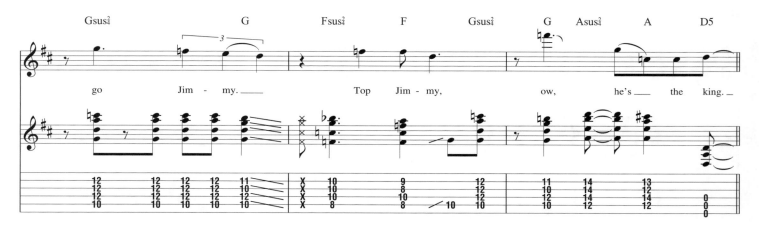

go Jim - my. _____ Top Jim - my, ow, he's ___ the king. _

Outro
Free time

Falsetto: Oh, Jimmy!

*Vol. swells

**Rapidly roll vol. knob back and forth in a sixteenth-note rhythm to simulate a Leslie effect.

Pitch: A
       E

from *Fair Warning*

Unchained

Words and Music by David Lee Roth, Edward Van Halen, Alex Van Halen and Michael Anthony

Gtr. 1: Drop D tuning, down 1/2 step:
(low to high) Db-Ab-Db-Gb-Bb-Eb

Gtr. 2: Tune down 1/2 step:
(low to high) Eb-Ab-Db-Gb-Bb-Eb

Intro
Moderate Rock ♩ = 138

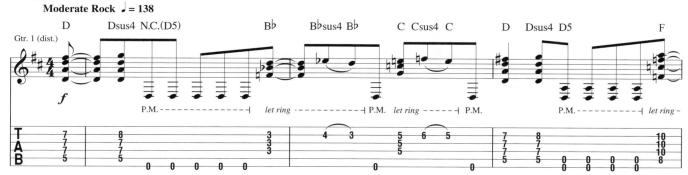

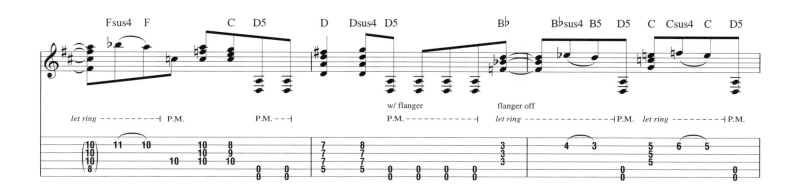

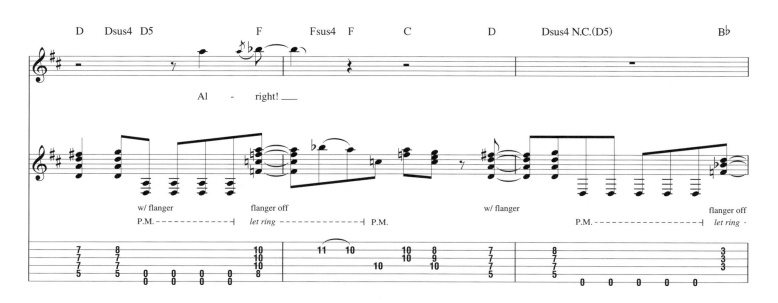

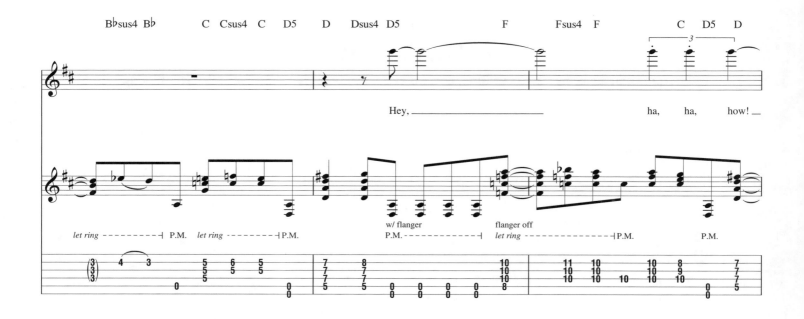

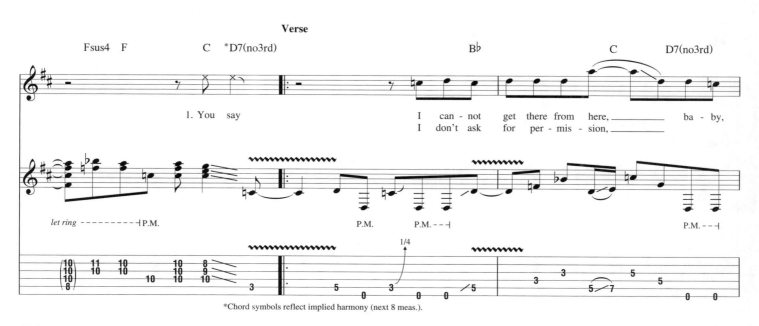

*Chord symbols reflect implied harmony (next 8 meas.).

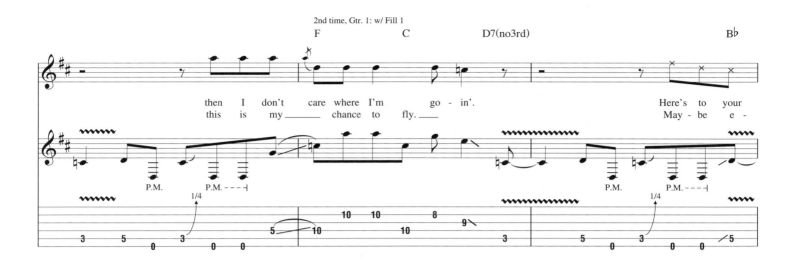

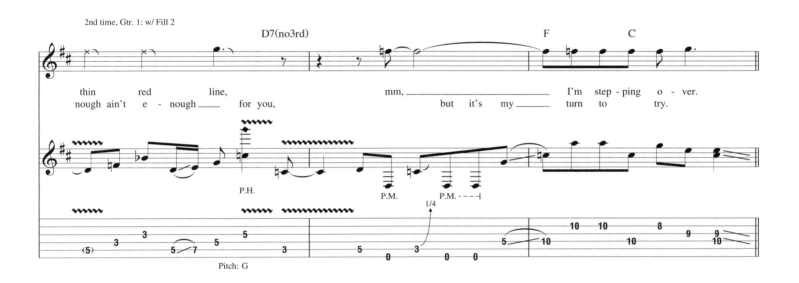

189

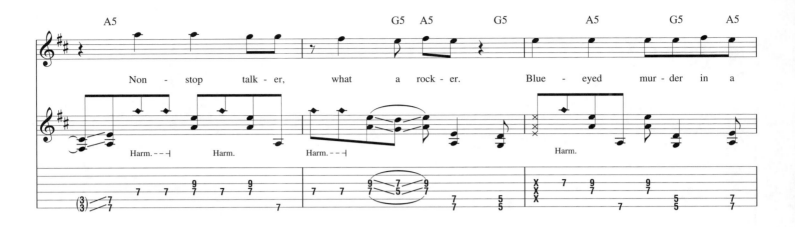

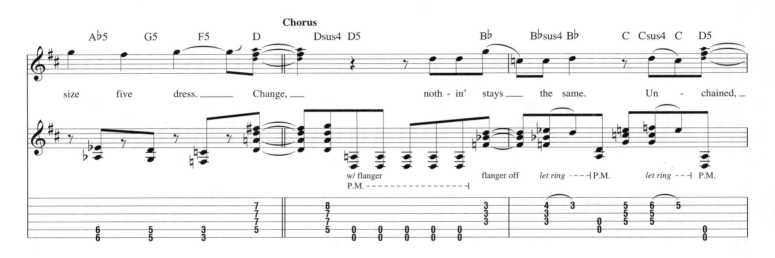

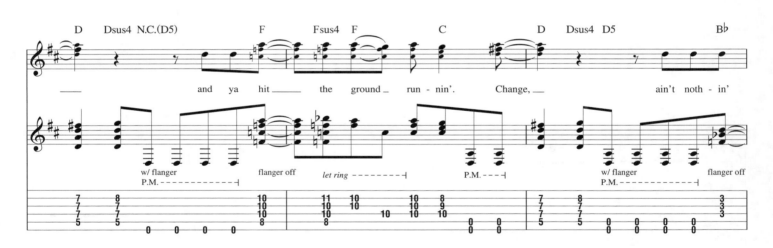

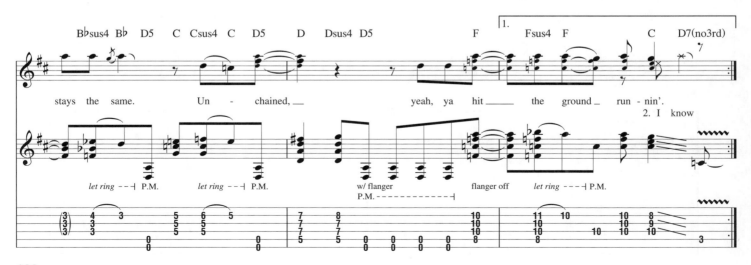

2.

Guitar Solo

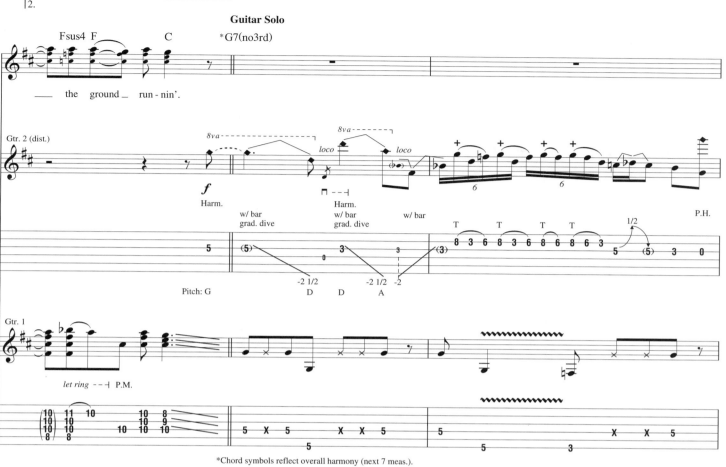

the ground run-nin'.

*Chord symbols reflect overall harmony (next 7 meas.).

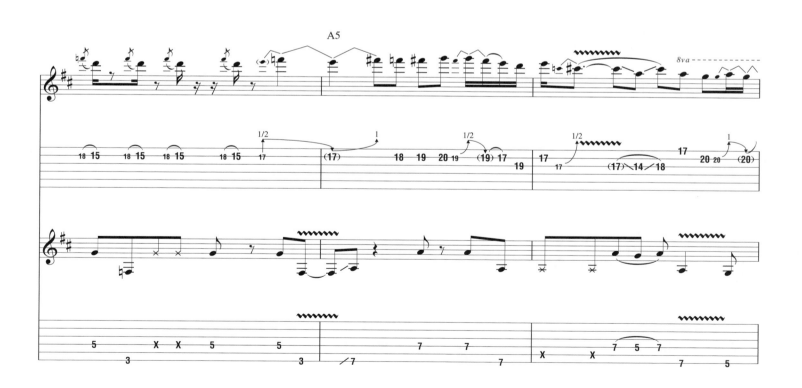

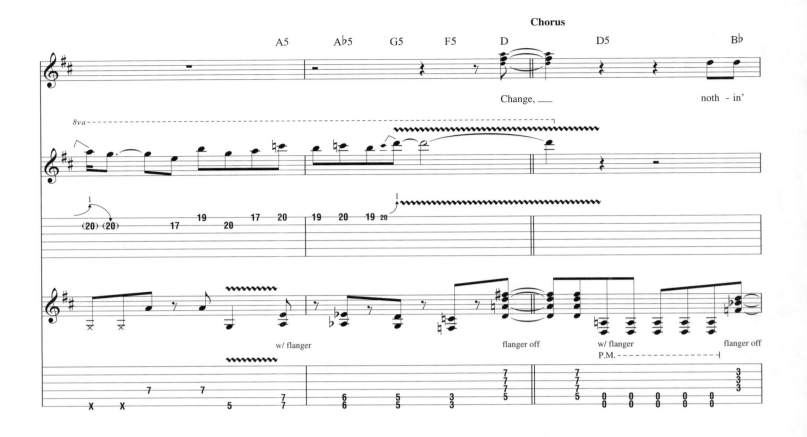

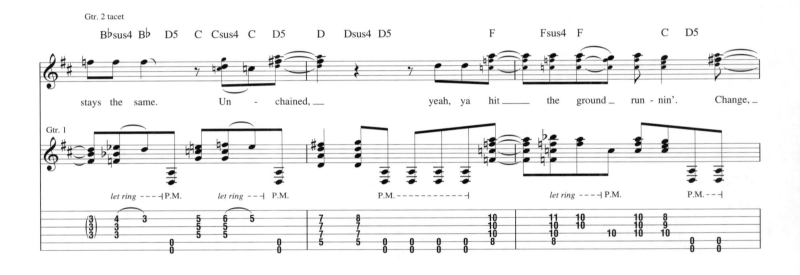

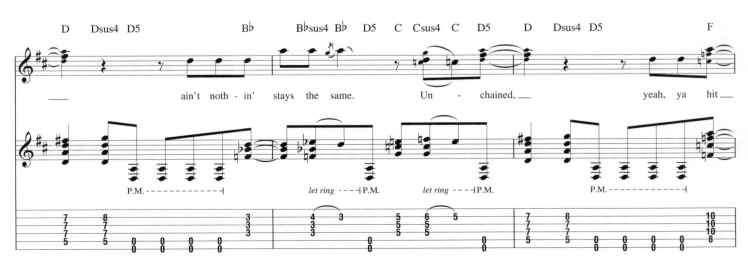

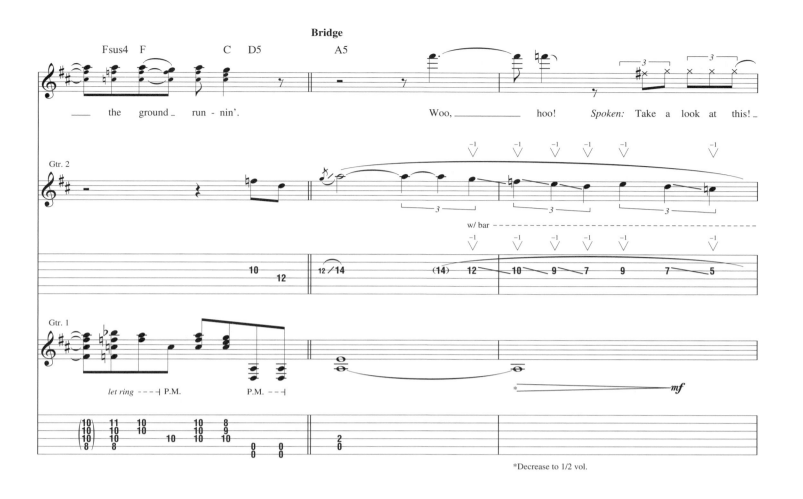

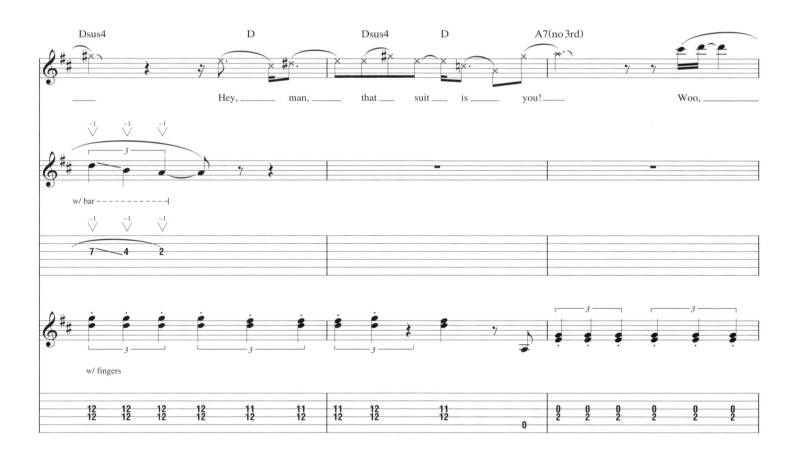

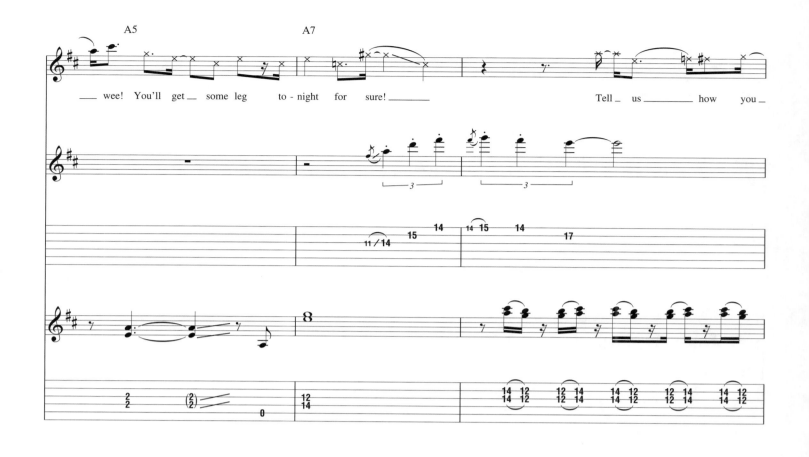

wee! You'll get ___ some leg to-night for sure! _____ Tell ___ us _____ how you ___

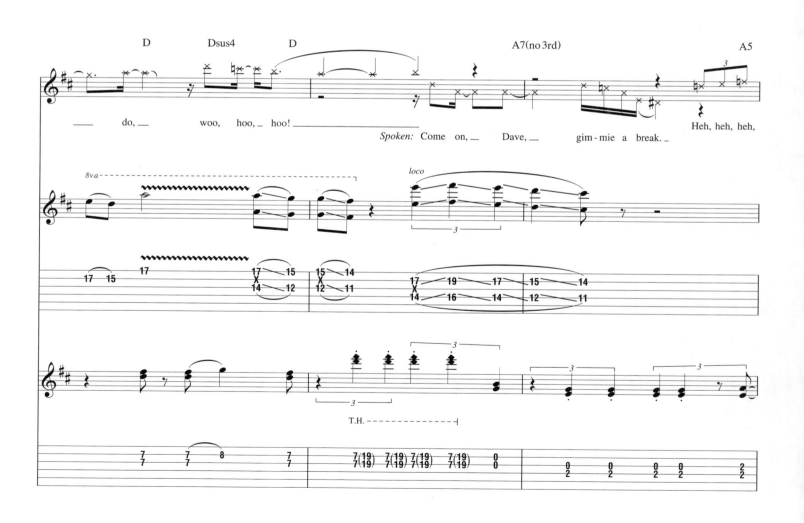

___ do, ___ woo, hoo, ___ hoo! _____ Heh, heh, heh,

Spoken: Come on, ___ Dave, ___ gim-mie a break. ___

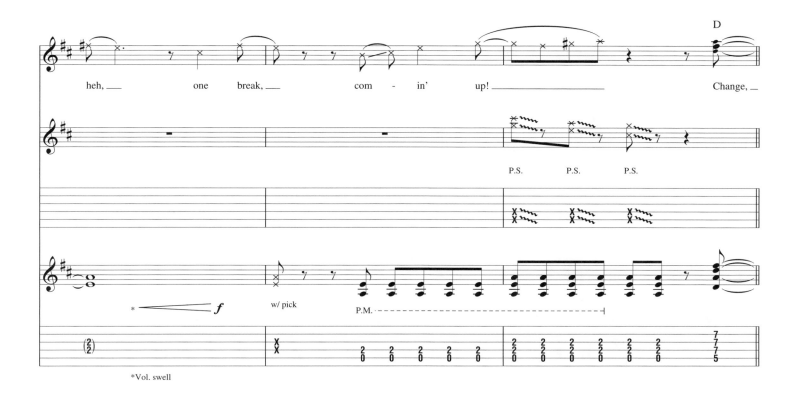

Chorus

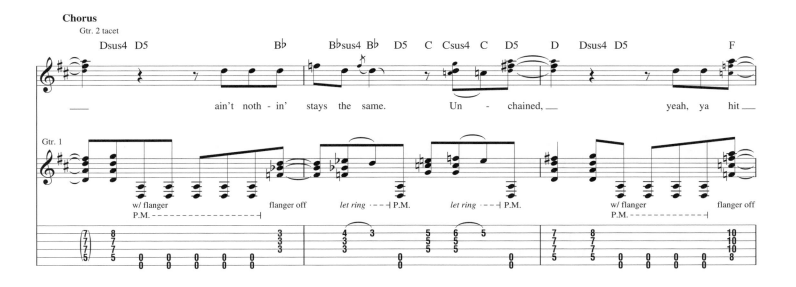

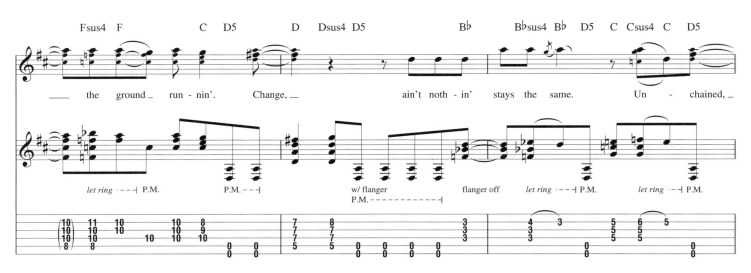

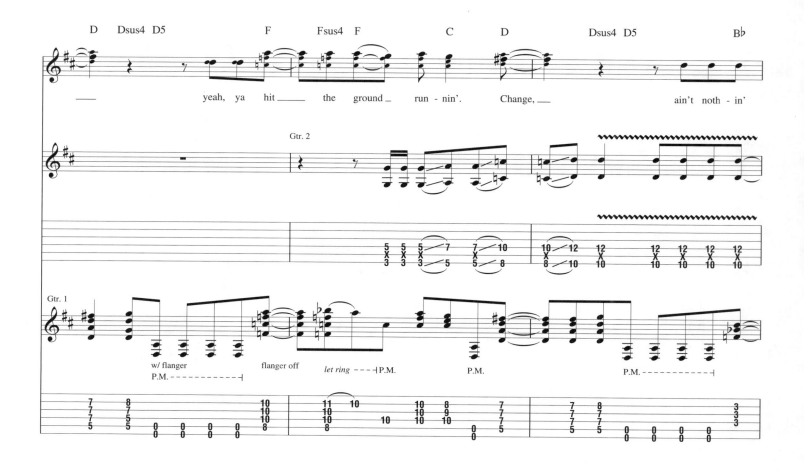

yeah, ya hit ___ the ground ___ run - nin'. Change, ___ ain't noth - in'

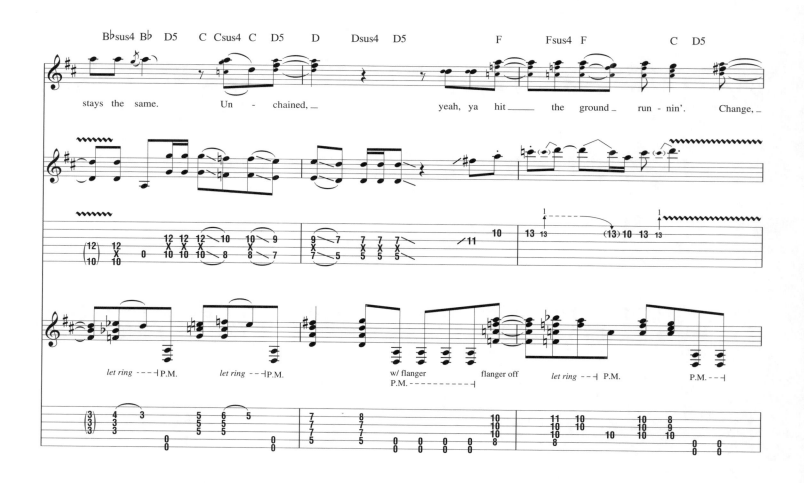

stays the same. Un - chained, ___ yeah, ya hit ___ the ground ___ run - nin'. Change, ___

*Decrease to 3/4 vol.
**Strum w/ R.H. pinky.

Guitar Notation Legend

Guitar music can be notated three different ways: on a *musical staff*, in *tablature*, and in *rhythm slashes*.

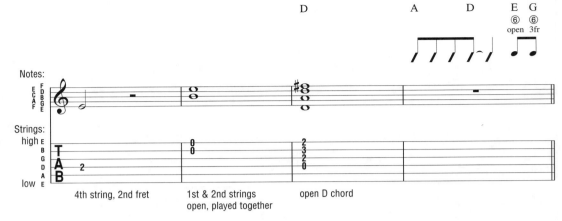

RHYTHM SLASHES are written above the staff. Strum chords in the rhythm indicated. Use the chord diagrams found at the top of the first page of the transcription for the appropriate chord voicings. Round noteheads indicate single notes.

THE MUSICAL STAFF shows pitches and rhythms and is divided by bar lines into measures. Pitches are named after the first seven letters of the alphabet.

TABLATURE graphically represents the guitar fingerboard. Each horizontal line represents a string, and each number represents a fret.

Notes:

Strings:

high E
B
G
D
A
low E

4th string, 2nd fret

1st & 2nd strings open, played together

open D chord

Definitions for Special Guitar Notation

HALF-STEP BEND: Strike the note and bend up 1/2 step.

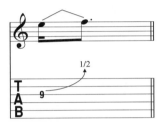

WHOLE-STEP BEND: Strike the note and bend up one step.

GRACE NOTE BEND: Strike the note and immediately bend up as indicated.

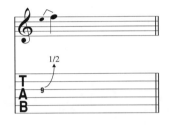

SLIGHT (MICROTONE) BEND: Strike the note and bend up 1/4 step.

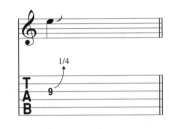

BEND AND RELEASE: Strike the note and bend up as indicated, then release back to the original note. Only the first note is struck.

PRE-BEND: Bend the note as indicated, then strike it.

PRE-BEND AND RELEASE: Bend the note as indicated. Strike it and release the bend back to the original note.

UNISON BEND: Strike the two notes simultaneously and bend the lower note up to the pitch of the higher.

VIBRATO: The string is vibrated by rapidly bending and releasing the note with the fretting hand.

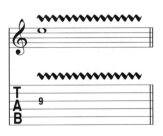

WIDE VIBRATO: The pitch is varied to a greater degree by vibrating with the fretting hand.

HAMMER-ON: Strike the first (lower) note with one finger, then sound the higher note (on the same string) with another finger by fretting it without picking.

PULL-OFF: Place both fingers on the notes to be sounded. Strike the first note and without picking, pull the finger off to sound the second (lower) note.

LEGATO SLIDE: Strike the first note and then slide the same fret-hand finger up or down to the second note. The second note is not struck.

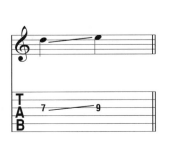

SHIFT SLIDE: Same as legato slide, except the second note is struck.

TRILL: Very rapidly alternate between the notes indicated by continuously hammering on and pulling off.

TAPPING: Hammer ("tap") the fret indicated with the pick-hand index or middle finger and pull off to the note fretted by the fret hand.

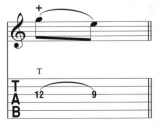

NATURAL HARMONIC: Strike the note while the fret-hand lightly touches the string directly over the fret indicated.

PINCH HARMONIC: The note is fretted normally and a harmonic is produced by adding the edge of the thumb or the tip of the index finger of the pick hand to the normal pick attack.

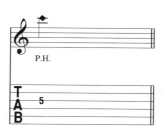

HARP HARMONIC: The note is fretted normally and a harmonic is produced by gently resting the pick hand's index finger directly above the indicated fret (in parentheses) while the pick hand's thumb or pick assists by plucking the appropriate string.

PICK SCRAPE: The edge of the pick is rubbed down (or up) the string, producing a scratchy sound.

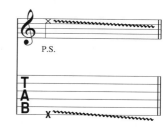

MUFFLED STRINGS: A percussive sound is produced by laying the fret hand across the string(s) without depressing, and striking them with the pick hand.

PALM MUTING: The note is partially muted by the pick hand lightly touching the string(s) just before the bridge.

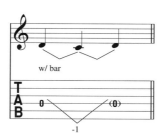

RAKE: Drag the pick across the strings indicated with a single motion.

TREMOLO PICKING: The note is picked as rapidly and continuously as possible.

ARPEGGIATE: Play the notes of the chord indicated by quickly rolling them from bottom to top.

VIBRATO BAR DIVE AND RETURN: The pitch of the note or chord is dropped a specified number of steps (in rhythm), then returned to the original pitch.

VIBRATO BAR SCOOP: Depress the bar just before striking the note, then quickly release the bar.

VIBRATO BAR DIP: Strike the note and then immediately drop a specified number of steps, then release back to the original pitch.

Additional Musical Definitions

> (accent)	• Accentuate note (play it louder).	
^ (accent)	• Accentuate note with great intensity.	
. (staccato)	• Play the note short.	
⊓	• Downstroke	
V	• Upstroke	

Rhy. Fig. • Label used to recall a recurring accompaniment pattern (usually chordal).

Riff • Label used to recall composed, melodic lines (usually single notes) which recur.

Fill • Label used to identify a brief melodic figure which is to be inserted into the arrangement.

Rhy. Fill • A chordal version of a Fill.

tacet • Instrument is silent (drops out).

D.S. al Coda • Go back to the sign (𝄋), then play until the measure marked "***To Coda***," then skip to the section labelled "**Coda**."

D.C. al Fine • Go back to the beginning of the song and play until the measure marked "***Fine***" (end).

• Repeat measures between signs.

• When a repeated section has different endings, play the first ending only the first time and the second ending only the second time.

NOTE: Tablature numbers in parentheses mean:
1. The note is being sustained over a system (note in standard notation is tied), or
2. The note is sustained, but a new articulation (such as a hammer-on, pull-off, slide or vibrato) begins, or
3. The note is a barely audible "ghost" note (note in standard notation is also in parentheses).

RECORDED VERSIONS®
The Best Note-For-Note Transcriptions Available

ALL BOOKS INCLUDE TABLATURE